Contents

MANAGING
EXPORT
DISTRIBUTION

Gary Davies PhD, DIC, BSc, ARSM, MSExec

HEINEMANN : LONDON

William Heinemann Ltd
10 Upper Grosvenor Street, London W1X 9PA

LONDON   MELBOURNE   TORONTO
JOHANNESBURG   AUCKLAND

First published 1984 in association with
Seabourne Express Limited
3–5 Thames Road, Barking, Essex IG11 0HB

ISBN 434 90298 5

Photoset in Great Britain by
Wilmaset, Birkenhead, Merseyside
Printed in Great Britain by
Redwood Burn Limited, Trowbridge

Part Three
The International Distribution Industry

Foreword

Distribution often appears on the Board Room agenda. The words 'international distribution' may also be included. All too often the item is put forward as a problem area, an area of high cost and few benefits.

Attitudes towards distribution as a business function are nevertheless changing. More importance is being given to better delivery performance. The status of the distribution manager is increasing. Yet all this is happening very slowly, with a great emphasis on trying to save money on the very high costs involved in moving goods internationally rather than on the probability of improving sales and profits by providing the best, or at least the most appropriate, service to the importer.

It has never failed to astound me how much emphasis within firms is given to the marketing of a product compared to its distribution and whether the product advertising was particularly eye-catching. Yet in many instances the percentages of the selling price spent on both are comparable. The likelihood of losing a customer is surely more dependent upon whether he gets his goods in good order and in good time than whether or not the packaging has been printed in full colour?

National and international bodies have commented on the need for greater professionalism in the way companies approach distribution. It is no secret that my own company Seabourne Express has been active in promoting a more professional approach to freighting for many years, beginning with the introduction of the first surface express service in Europe in 1970. It is therefore both timely and appropriate that *Managing Export Distribution* has been written and for Seabourne to offer its full support to the text.

This book will be an important reference manual, full, as it is, of new ideas and solid management approaches. It should be as much a part of a company's approach to better and more profitable trade as any of the modern aids to exporting cited in its pages.

Clive Bourne
Managing Director
Seabourne Express Limited

Preface

Managing Export Distribution has been written both for the practitioner and for the student of international distribution. My objective has been to interpret the results from an extensive research programme conducted by various people at Manchester Polytechnic since 1977. During this time nearly 200 trading companies having been visited in Europe and over 3000 firms and individuals have been surveyed. Valuable information has also been gathered from other countries and continents, particularly the USA.

It would have been a breach of faith with the many practising managers who have given their time and shared their expertise to have written a totally academic text. This may well have been of great value to theoreticians – but it would have been of limited value to practitioners and potential practitioners. Instead I have aimed to produce a book which bridges the gap between theory and practice. Theory has to have its place to provide a manager with a structure in his job and to explain the complexity of practice to the student, but without practical examples theory can remain isolated and seemingly irrelevant. Hence most of the main points I have tried to make are illustrated by real examples, sometimes disguised, of day-to-day practical problems.

The book is in three parts. Part One puts distribution management into the context of successful exporting and importing. Part Two concerns itself in detail with the management of International distribution. The final part describes the structure of the international distribution industry and how the changes in that industry affect the trader.

Finally I would like to record my sincere thanks to all those who have helped make this book possible. A list of names would mean another chapter; the five researchers over the years in Manchester; the institutions, organizations and companies who have funded or sponsored their work; the publishers of this text and those of my articles; the professional societies and their members who have provided data; the sponsoring company for this text; my family and friends for their encouragement; other authors for permission to use their work; and the very many individuals, without whose co-operation nothing would ever have appeared in print. Instead of a list of names I offer a simple thank you. If this book is judged to have any value by those who read it, it is to their credit and not to mine.

Gary Davies
Poynton, Cheshire

PART ONE
Management and export distribution

1
International business and international distribution

More and more of the goods we buy each year are made totally or partially in another country. The proportion of world output which is traded between countries has grown steadily. It is no longer adequate to think of the major manufacturing companies as belonging to one country. Today's multinational corporation knows few boundaries. A component company in one country can supply many countries in the same corporation around the world.

Since the middle of the 1970s the cost of moving goods has spiralled as fuel prices have leapt. These same increases in oil prices have encouraged governments to stimulate growth in export volume to balance the cost of dearer imports. Rising oil costs also contributed to the world-wide recession in the 1980s. The result is that competition for declining world markets has increased at a time when the costs of serving the same markets have risen.

Management attention has, consequently, become focused on the costs of distribution and especially on the costs of international distribution. Estimates in various texts of the cost of transportation and documentation are that it amounts to between 15% and 40% of the delivered price of exported goods. The range in proportion of the selling price accounted for by distribution costs is, in practice, even wider. A British pharmaceutical company budgets only 0.2% of its selling price for distribution costs within Europe and 2% worldwide. Another British company selling plastic mouldings has to mark up their domestic selling price 100% on one large selling item to Middle Eastern markets to cover transport costs alone. Raw materials can have an even higher percentage contribution to selling price from distribution costs.

The importance of price in export success

A number of countries, including Britain and the USA, were particularly conscious of their falling share of world trade in manufactured goods during the 1970s. Some of the explanation for these trends lay in the emergence of developing countries as exporters of manufactured and semi-manufactured goods as well as raw materials. But the success of some developed countries, notably West Germany and Japan, encouraged other developed nations to look closely for reasons for their own relative lack of success. The list of factors which are claimed to contribute to a declining share of trade is seemingly endless. They range from lack of language ability to a moral reluctance to indulge in petty bribery, from poor industrial relations to poor product quality. Fundamentally the various reasons fall into two broad groups:

Price-related factors	Selling price, exchange rates, tariff barriers, distribution costs etc.
Non-price-related factors	Delivery times, service levels, product quality, marketing ability, etc.

One analysis has thrown some doubt on the contribution that price advantage makes in international trade. The contribution that a competitive price can make will vary by the type of product being considered. A buyer of raw materials or basic foodstuffs might be persuaded to switch sources over a price difference of a few pennies. A buyer, or distributor, of more complex manufactured products may be much more concerned about non-price factors and need a large price difference to encourage him to switch to a supplier offering poor service.

Economists in the British National Economic Development

Office (NEDO) plotted the share of world trade in certain manufactured goods achieved by Britain over the 1960s and 1970s. They compared this with similar graphs for Britain's main competitors in the European Economic Community (EEC), France and West Germany.[1] For the same product groups they also plotted the changes in the average value per tonne. This gives a crude but workable measure of the prices being charged for these products which can then be compared with those of another country.

The type of results they produced is shown schematically in Figures 1(a) and (b). While Britain was gaining a relative price advantage her share of trade was declining. The price advantage being gained by the progressive devaluation of the pound was not enough to increase sales to provide the same, or a higher, income.

In the early 1980s the application of monetarist policies, including high interest rates by the British Government, coupled with a recovery in international confidence in the British economy, saw the pound harden against other leading currencies. The boom in imports and slump in exports expected by some did not occur. Conversely, total export value held well for some time.

The NEDO economists concluded that whatever the problem had been that lay at the root of Britain's relative lack of success in world markets, it was not a problem associated with being overpriced.

Non-price factors can be much more important than price factors in a country's export success and it is likely that the same will be true for individual manufacturers. While it is perhaps inevitable that management attention will increasingly focus on the costs of distribution, it is essential to realize that cost is not necessarily the most important aspect of distribution.

Nevertheless much of this book is concerned with management techniques that are about controlling cost. Freight costs between European and North American markets, for example, often exceed the more talked about barriers to trade of tariffs. A few percent saved on a freight bill can significantly affect profitability and sales.

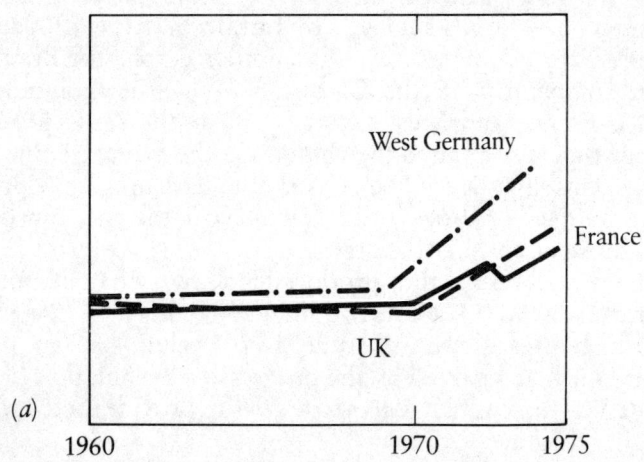

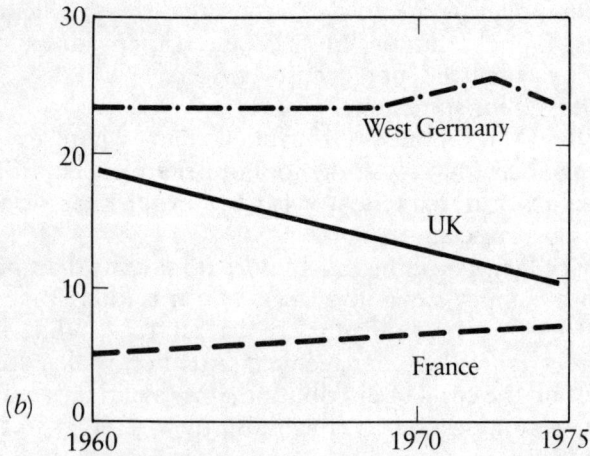

Figure 1   NEDO study indicating the importance of non-price factors. (*a*)
Average value per tonne exports of engineering products; (*b*)
Percentage share of main industrial countries exports of engineering products. *Source*: schematic representation of Figures 2 and 3,
p. 1a *The UK's performance in export markets – some evidence
from international trade data*, David Connell, NEDO: London,
1979.

Distribution as a non-price factor

A buyer approaching a retailer, wholesaler, agent or manufacturer wants to be able to purchase immediately or to a date which suits him as a buyer. The marketing systems of consumer goods companies are geared to provide a high level of retail distribution and availability. More than one study has demonstrated the basic lack of brand loyalty in the typical consumer when faced with an out of stock position on his, or her, regular brand. Consumer product companies allocate considerable resources (sales and merchandising staff, trade promotions, high inventory levels) in their efforts to ensure that a potential customer has at least the option of buying their product.

In industrial markets the industrial buyer is more used to having to buy to order than from stock. Many manufacturers of custom-built equipment have no reason to hold stock of anything but spare parts and components. Instead of goods the buyer is offered a delivery promise.

Some companies experience difficulties in meeting the delivery times they promise. Sometimes the delivery promise is clearly far too ambitious. This can be quite prevalent in export business where salespeople's perceptions of the order processing and transport times on international orders are often much shorter than can be achieved in practice. Sometimes the firm's own internal system is at fault, or perhaps there is no system to speak of for co-ordinating delivery promises with lead times.

There is some evidence of the relative importance of delivery times in exporting. Significantly it is one of the few studies ever conducted on exporting *customers* rather than on exporting *firms*. The survey asked firms selling British products in continental Europe to rank a list of factors that could be limiting their sales of British products. Within the EEC 'delivery' was ranked first and in non-EEC countries it was ranked second to 'tariff barriers'.[2] Another study, at about the same time, included a measure of the delivery times actually achieved by French, German, and British firms. Those for British firms fell only slightly behind those for German firms and were comparable with those of French firms.[3] Both surveys were conducted in the late 1970s.

During this period British industry was convinced that it had a reputation for late delivery. The European study seemed to confirm that a delivery problem existed but the comparative study implied that the problem was not associated with overlong delivery times but rather with overambitious and therefore unreliable delivery promises. In Chapter 7 the influence of reliability on the purchase of transport services is highlighted. There is little doubt that unreliable delivery promises can discourage the repurchase of any product.

Delivery performance is then almost certainly a key factor in successful marketing and, as a non-price factor, is one which is worthy of particular evaluation in exporting. Companies selling high repeat order products (consumer goods, industrial components, raw materials, etc.) will differ from those selling custom-built products on the areas of relevant concern. The former will be concerned mainly with optimizing their order processing and distribution systems which together constitute their international logistics system. The latter will be equally, or more concerned with their systems for predicting and controlling design and manufacturing lead times. This distinction between high repeat order products, which are potentially available ex-stock, and custom-built products is one that should be borne in mind throughout this book. It is both easier and more desirable for companies involved with the former type of product to evolve many of the management approaches that will be outlined.

Domestic and international logistics

International trade is generally regarded as being more complex than domestic trade. Products have to be redesigned, there are language barriers and tariff barriers. From a logistics perspective certain aspects are more complex, others are more straightforward.

Documentation is certainly more complex with information needed for up to fifty commercial procedures involving perhaps fifteen separate parties. Documentation can be daunting for the smaller firm which is considering whether or not to begin exporting. In one study, small American firms were asked why other small firms were not exporting.[4] The five most important perceptions were:

1 Lack of exposure to other cultures
2 The large domestic market
3 Lack of staff time
4 The paperwork and management of export operations
5 Different safety and quality standards

while the same firms ranked their own problems with exporting as:

1 Paperwork
2 Selecting a reliable distributor
3 Competitive disadvantages due to non-tariff barriers
4 Honouring Letters of Credit
5 Communication with foreign customers.

Paperwork is certainly seen as a problem in international trade. Because of the inter-relationship between trade and transportation paperwork, the responsibility for both is usually combined and linked with the responsibility for purchasing international freight. This wide-ranging role is one major difference between domestic and international distribution management.

While it is more complex, one benefit to distribution management in international business on high repeat order goods is that export orders tend to be much larger than domestic orders. The reason is that a majority of such exports are to an overseas subsidiary or agent who is buying for stock or grouping smaller orders into one large order from the supplying manufacturer.

This last observation is worth restating in another way as it emphasizes the subtley different role that distribution plays in international marketing.

As firms evolve into international companies they change from being primarily domestic manufacturers who occasionally export directly to a limited number of customers, to employing a full-time agent, to establishing a permanent sales office of their own in the overseas market, to operating a local manufacturing plant which could be supplied with some completed goods and some semi-manufactures from the parent company.

Once the firm stops selling directly to the foreign buyer and sells via an agent or its own subsidiary the parent company loses the responsibility for not only sales but often advertising and promotion and other elements in their 'marketing mix' in the overseas market. The role of the parent company, in day-to-day relationships, is of supplier of products and components. Distribution and order processing become much more prominent and logistics can become even the *most* important element in the parent company's international marketing effort.

The status of distribution management

Peter Drucker, probably the best-known writer on management topics, once labelled distribution as the 'economy's dark continent'.[5] Salary surveys on those managers concerned with distribution tend to confirm the lack of attention paid in the past to all elements of distribution. Comparing the results of one survey of professional international distribution managers (or shipping managers as they are called) in Britain with a salary survey of all British managers demonstrated that this generalization can be extended from domestic to international management. In 1979/80, in Britain, shipping managers' salaries averaged approximately one-half of those paid to all management.[6] Very few shipping managers in this survey were graduates. Most had left full-time education at an early age although many had continued with their studies on part-time courses.

In the trade press serving the freighting industry, shipping managers often compare their industrial role unfavourably with that of other line management functions, especially purchasing. Strauss documented the rise of the purchasing agent or buyer in America during the 1960s. He concentrated on the way in which purchasing agents 'sold' the importance of their role to senior management.[7] It is all too easy to mistake professionalism for the interfunctionary rivalry of which Strauss accuses the purchasing agent. Senior management is unlikely to be impressed by demands for better pay and fringe benefits from any management group, no matter how valid their case, if that case is based upon claims of being underpaid relative to other management functions. Paying higher salaries for the same job is hardly an objective which will appeal to senior management. It is better to argue the case for more responsibility to be added to an original role. The widened responsibility will justify a higher remuneration.

It is the author's view that the international distribution role has been severely undervalued by the majority of firms and that both line and staff managers have all too frequently ignored the possibility of building a more efficient and profitable international business by developing this function.

The trend over the last two decades has been for traders to become more involved in their own international freight forwarding. Great strides have been made in the development of documentation systems and computerized order processing systems. Physical distribution has become simpler and more reliable. However management thought has lagged behind these developments in the evolution of management systems within the firm to take full advantage of these changes.

Senior management cannot afford to ignore statements such as the one quoted here from independent bodies such as the UK's National Economic Development Council:[8] 'There is still a tendency to produce and sell first and think about movement later but physical distribution should enter into the long-and medium-term planning of every export activity.'

Glossary

Few terms are universally accepted in international distribution throughout any one country let alone throughout the world. The following terms and meanings will be used throughout the text.

Bill of lading   The international document (ships

	bill rather than a general despatch note).
Consignee	The individual or company responsible for receiving the goods, usually the buyer.
Consignor	The individual or company responsible for despatch (also referred to as the shipper).
Freight forwarder	The international freight forwarder, who, in Europe, may also be a Customs Agent and secondary carrier.
Logistics management	The management of a system designed to optimize profitability by improving customer service. It will normally include distribution and order processing.
Secondary carrier	A company combining international forwarding with ownership of transport equipment especially road vehicles and containers.
Shipping Manager/ Shipping department	The individual department or role responsible for international logistics.

Keypoints

1 Export distribution is a more complex task than domestic distribution.
2 Delivery is a major non-price factor in export success and one which can dominate a company's export marketing mix.
3 The status of shipping management is low but the function could be built upon in taking better account of the role of distribution in exporting.

References and further reading

1 NEDO Discussion paper 6 on the UK Performance in Export Markets, 1979.

2 British Chamber of Commerce in Continental Europe, Paris, 1979.
3 *Barclays Bank Export Development Report*, Barclays International, 1978.
4 RABINO, SAMUEL '*An examination of Barriers to Exporting Encountered by Small Manufacturing Companies*'.
5 DRUCKER, PETER 'The Economy's Dark Continent', *Fortune*, April 1962.
6 DAVIES G. J. and GRAY, R. '*Who Buys International Freight Services*' (Maclean Hunter: London, 1980).
7 STRAUSS, G. 'A case study of Purchasing Agents' *Human Organisation* Vol. 23, 2, 1964.
8 NEDO 'Trading with Europe' London, 1977.

WENTWORTH, FELIX and CHRISTOPHER, MARTIN (eds) '*Managing International Distribution*' (Gower, Aldershot, 1979).
TOOKEY, DOUGLAS (ed) '*Physical Distribution for Export*' (Gower, Aldershot, 1971).
MURR, ALFRED '*Export/Import Traffic Management and Forwarding*' (Cornell Maritime Press, Maryland USA, 1979).
THOMAS MEADOWS LTD '*Understanding the Freight Business*' (London, 1979).
DAVIES, G. J. (ed) '*International Logistics*' (MCB Publications Ltd, Bradford, 1981).

2
Management concepts in international distribution

Line management and management tasks

Firms of any size are divided into different areas of specialization. The dominant basis for division is by various line management functions (Figure 2[a]). While this approach has many advantages it does have its disadvantages. Take for example the task of new product development. This involves the co-operation of research and development, marketing, accounts, purchasing and manufacturing. In other words new product development is a responsibility or task which cuts across traditional line functions.

Firms have attempted to minimize the problems of communication and co-ordination that can arise in product development in a number of ways, one of which is to appoint a new products co-ordinator who has both the responsibility and authority to co-ordinate the activities of members of the individual line functions.

In a similar way other tasks can be defined which also cut across management hierarchies. If these are important enough a logical development would be to establish a number of co-ordinators with cross line management authority. The company's organization chart ceases to look like a series of vertical lines and begins to look like a mesh or matrix (Figure 2[b]). The matrix approach to management was advocated strongly during the 1960s and 1970s by management theorists. Few firms adopted the approach and many who did abandoned the experiment.

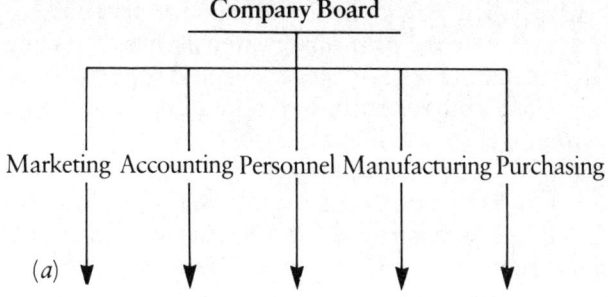

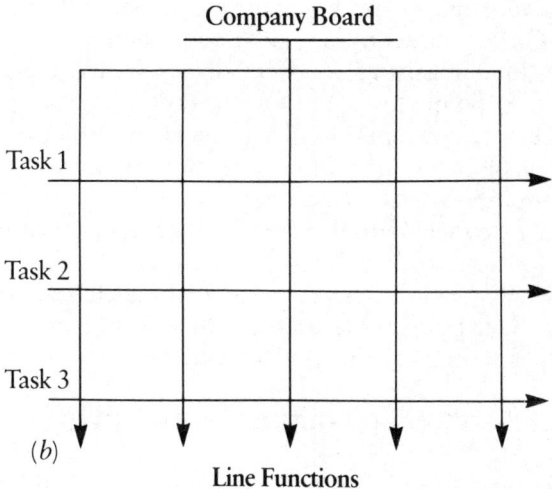

Figure 2(*a*)   Traditional line management; (*b*) The matrix organization.

One problem in using such an innovative approach is that, in practice, organizations are not lines and boxes on an organization chart: they are people. Radical change is often only grudgingly accepted but when it results in the establishment of two lines of authority competing for the time of individual managers, such a development can prove totally unacceptable.

The trend has been away from a matrix structure and more pragmatically to developing new management specialisms each with their own line of management as separate hierarchies within the firm. The responsibility to manage other cross-functional tasks has largely been delegated to committees of representatives from individual line functions, or to a senior manager in one line function.

Although the matrix approach may not be so fashionable today it has left us with the useful idea of looking for tasks which the firm needs to perform to survive which cut across line management responsibilities. One way or another these tasks have to be managed.

Each of these tasks can be regarded as a system, a system of related activities which need to be co-ordinated. One way of analysing a business is to define the systems that do or should operate. Quite frequently a task is being performed without co-ord'nation. Imposing a system or a systematic approach will improve the management of that task.

Management concepts should, to be of any practical value, be capable of being translated into one or more workable systems within a firm. This chapter outlines a number of management concepts that have proven beneficial in managing distribution and evaluates which can be applied to international distribution. Each involves different ways of looking at distribution as a system rather than, as it is so often regarded, as a series of unassociated components.

Physical distribution management (PDM)

All the distribution activities of a firm interact to influence the total cost of distribution to the firm and the level of service to the customer. Early attempts to develop the PDM concept emphasized the point that transport costs, warehousing costs, and packaging costs should be regarded as one total distribution cost. Very quickly the necessity of including the effect on customer service was included so that the PDM objective is normally stated as 'getting the right goods to the right places at the right time for the least cost'.

All too often a company's ideas on PDM have centred on reducing costs. Assertions that '40% or more of our selling price was at one time a distribution cost', while concentrating attention on physical distribution, have tended to emphasize the effect that better control on costs can have on company profits.

Less time has been spent emphasizing the relationship between better delivery times (at increased cost) and increased sales. Freight buyers are generally disposed to pay more for a better service, and so are purchasers of any products. You can check this statement the next time you are deciding whether to place an order for a washing machine. One make of washing machine is out of stock and has a delivery time of six weeks. Another similar model is immediately available. Ask yourself how much *more* you are willing to pay for the model in stock.

Availability has a value which can, however inaccurately, be quantified in terms of money. Stock levels and order processing times are then very much associated with physical distribution costs but increased stocks and reduced order processing times cost money to achieve. It is possible to estimate what availability a firm should seek to provide to maximize its own profitability. This is discussed in the next section.

The physical distribution system has been described as a series of intermeshed cogs carrying the goods to the customer. However the system is not only about transport, warehousing, packaging and order processing. There is another flow or system in the opposite direction, of information. The distribution function has come to be regarded as the best source of management information on the state of business of the firm.

Current business can be measured in four main ways: quotations given, orders received, orders despatched, invoices paid. Goods are normally invoiced at the time of despatch and as a company legally makes its profit when the customer is invoiced rather than when he pays, orders despatched is a doubly good measure of the business position. It is superior to orders received because of the number of orders which may be cancelled, modified or even duplicated.

Despatch data can also be analysed to provide data on business by market sector, geographical area, individual customer, drop size and drop frequency. Modern computer analysis makes it relatively easy to calculate or estimate the profit a company makes out of each customer or distributor. Some customers who order frequent, small quantities of low profit margin products may well be costing a company money. This idea of calculating 'customer account profitability' is feasible as a result of the data available from a PDM system. While these techniques are often applied to home sales they can be equally revealing on export business given the high cost of freight minimums associated with international freight.

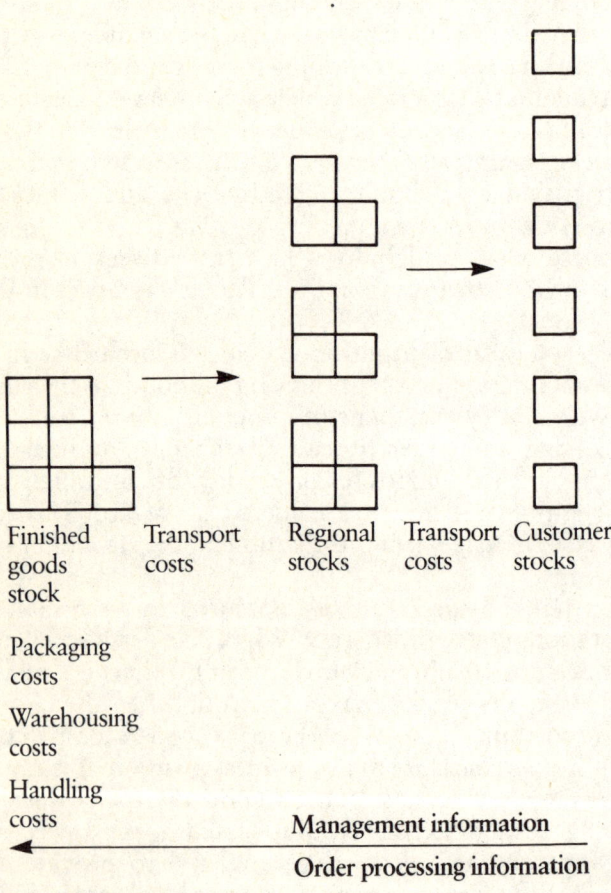

Finished   Transport   Regional   Transport   Customer
goods   costs   stocks   costs   stocks
stock

Packaging
costs

Warehousing
costs

Handling
costs   Management information
                          ←————————————————————————
                              Order processing information

Figure 3   The PDM system.

The PDM system can be represented diagrammatically as in Figure 3. Goods flow in one direction, information in the other.

Materials management

Inventory costs, handling costs and order processing costs are not only incurred in the outward movement of goods to the customer. Because a company buys, as well as sells, it will incur all these costs at both ends of the firm. Goods are moved during production. Materials management should also be regarded as a business system. As with PDM it is something of a balancing act, this time minimizing stock levels and maximizing production flexibility.

In the international context some shipping departments are concerned solely with importing raw materials or commodities such as timber and wine for their companies. Their customer is the manufacturing or bottling plant whom they have to serve at the minimum inventory cost to the company while keeping the purchasing cost from their suppliers also at a low level, by not incurring too high transport costs or buying in uneconomic quantities.

Materials management can be a more dynamic system in that purchasing departments may well see a commercial advantage in buying certain products at different times because of imminent price rises or projected scarcity. Nevertheless materials management and PDM share the common theme of the movement of things, of raw materials, components, semi-finished product and finished stock. Side by side the two systems demonstrate the movement of goods and materials into and through the firm and on to the customer. Both concepts emphasize the minimization of costs by reducing inventory levels, transport costs and the like, both emphasize the reconciliation of this with maximizing customer satisfaction, be it the buyers of the company's products or the production unit as the customer for the purchasing function.

Recognizing this commonality of purpose has lead to the definition of the 'logistics concept' which combines the PDM and materials management ideas.

The logistics concept

The term 'logistics' has been applied to a number of areas. To some it is synonymous with distribution. As a management concept it is a much broader idea. It emphasizes the task of moving materials into and through the firm and onwards to the customer Figure 4. Some authors on the subject include at

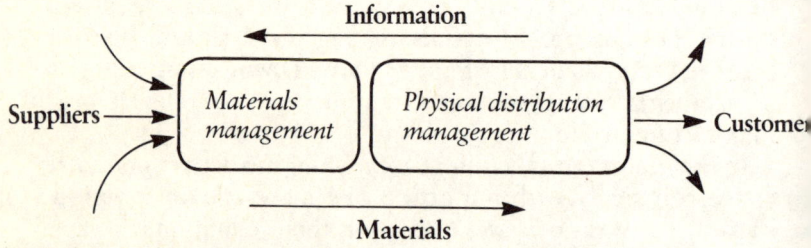

Figure 4   The logistics concept.

least part of the marketing function, specifically sales, within the logistics task. With its emphasis on optimizing costs and customer service levels to the greatest benefit to the firm it has an obvious commonality with marketing in the objective of improving customer service. However the key points which differentiate the two perspectives are the words optimize and maximize when applied to customer service levels.

Marketing may be keen to increase stock levels to maximize service levels while distribution is being appraised on their ability to minimize stock holding. The logistics concept emphasizes the need to balance the two factors.

The logistics role is concerned with, or should be charged with, a number of decision areas:

Inventory	(quantity, order frequency, location, handling methods, warehouse management, order picking)
Transportation	(purchasing, route and mode decisions, own account or bought in)
Information	(management and control)
Packaging	(packing, packaging, unitization)

Service levels   (ex-stock availability, order processing times, transit times).

In many firms many of these areas will be the responsibility of individual line functions or will be highly dependent upon their role. In Chapter 3 the options open to the firm in the way it organizes its international distribution function are discussed. A fundamental decision is whether to create a separate logistics function in the firm as a new line function or to evolve a cross-line functional role to oversee this task, a matrix approach.

Logistics, as an academic subject and as a practical discipline, is a recent arrival on the management scene. Very little attention has been paid to developing the concept from its origins in strictly domestic trading to the international context.

International logistics

The task of moving goods through the firm and to the customer is as relevant to international as to national business. However the two environments do contain some marked dissimilarities.

In Chapter 1 the increased importance of order processing and transportation were emphasized especially where the firm is exporting to overseas subsidiaries. The need to optimize cost and service levels is still a valuable objective but the ultimate responsibility for end user service levels (the customer in the foreign market) is often not that of the manufacturer whose major role is to maintain wholesale stock levels with the subsidiary or agent.

Export order processing is complex and often associated with transport documentation. Transport costs are more expensive, transit times are longer and in dealing with underdeveloped markets are also less reliable. Firms deal with many more types of transport companies and many more individual transport concerns.

What is then the more important task for the exporter: the physical movement of goods or the movement of the *export order* including the procurement of transportation? The answer will vary depending upon the firm and its particular types of product and foreign market. However in most cases the more important task will be to process orders and procure transportation. Export logistics is best seen as the movement of the order into and through the firm and back to the customer in the form of goods. The traditional view of logistics, defined from a domestic context, with its emphasis on the movement of materials does not emphasize the key factor in exporting – moving the order.

On the import side where the firm is purchasing from foreign suppliers largely on an ex-works or FOB basis, the distribution role is very similar to the materials management role in domestic business (Figure 5).

The distinctions being argued are ones of degree rather than absolute differences. Firms who manufacture and market largely or exclusively within the European Community or the North American sub-continent will be managing domestic and international distribution systems which could be similar enough to combine into a single system. Firms trading

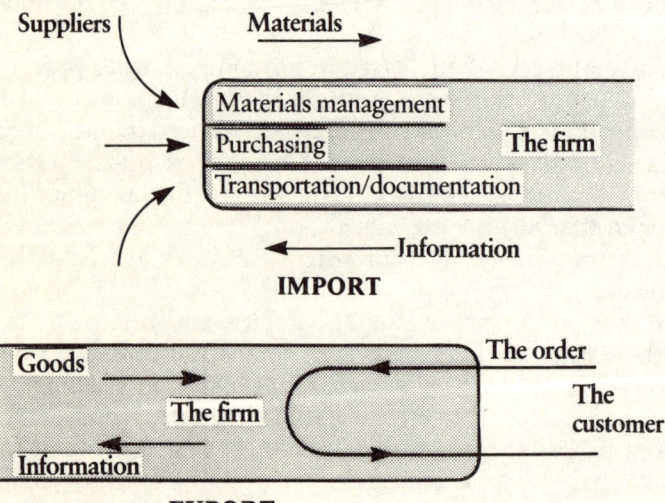

Figure 5   The international logistics concept.

worldwide will, on the other hand, be well advised to differentiate between domestic and international distribution and to decide how to accommodate the subtly different tasks involved in national and international logistics.

Concentrating, as we shall be, on export logistics the task of moving and export order through the firm is a cross-functional one. The responsibility for obtaining the order, if the company can influence this directly, is that of sales and marketing. If the sale is subject to a letter of credit, there is a legal role to check the terms and conditions of the letter. The credit status of a casual customer and the credit limit of a regular customer need checking, an accounting responsibility. Stock needs to be available, a domestic logistics function, or programmed into production, the responsibility of production scheduling. The order needs to be processed, a role that can be accounting or commercial services, and invoiced. The order finally needs documenting and commercial and transportation documentation brought together.

The commercial invoice will be presented in most transactions to the forwarder or the carrier. If the exporter is preparing any transport documentation or customs declaration himself these will need to be produced. An order under a letter of credit will usually require the bringing together of this document and a document to prove despatch, such as the bill of lading.

Export logistics is very much about co-ordination and the bringing together of traditionally diverse disciplines. Nevertheless shipping practitioners reading this text will recognize most of their responsibilities within the export logistics idea. Many shipping managers have this wide range of elements within their responsibility. All too few have the authority to optimize the logistics task. It may be seen already as a job but it is rarely seen as a management system worthy or senior management consideration.

Total distribution cost analysis

The need to trade-off service levels and logistics costs has been mentioned frequently throughout this chapter without much guidance as to how to achieve this balance. Needless to say there is no easy formula that can be applied.

For consumer products and for industrial components sold through a distribution system the effect of poor product availability is twofold. First, if the product is not on the shelf the customer could well buy a competitive product. Second, there is the possibility that the distributor will reduce the shelf space he allocates to a product with poor availability or decide to delist it. Distributors are likely to vary in their response to poor availability. In one survey 60% of buyers indicated they would never retaliate against the particular company who sponsored the research[1] if an item was not available. Of the 40% who would, half would take action after two lapses within six order periods, half after three lapses in six order periods.

Although any data attempting to predict future reactions is certainly suspect, this type of measurement does allow an estimation of the average cost of a supply failure. The cost is often a surprisingly high figure and dependant in part on the attitude of the individual customer to delivery delays.

For many industrial products the concept of immediate availability is irrelevant where the product is made to order. Here the lead time that a company can offer and achieve can be a critical factor. One way of representing this comes from some work by Stephensen[2]. He represents the probability of achieving an order as a function of the lead time offered by the supplier compared with the average lead time offered by all suppliers. An average lead time gives a 50:50 chance of obtaining the order. A small disadvantage on lead time represents a considerable drop in probability of success and vice versa. A very large relative advantage is needed to be sure of a sale.

The point was made in Chapter 1 that lead times and delivery promises are not necessarily the same. While an ambitious delivery promise can procure a first order, the buyer, having been let down, is unlikely to be so keen to re-order.

The penalty that a firm pays by allowing a service failure can be calculated with some degree of confidence at various levels

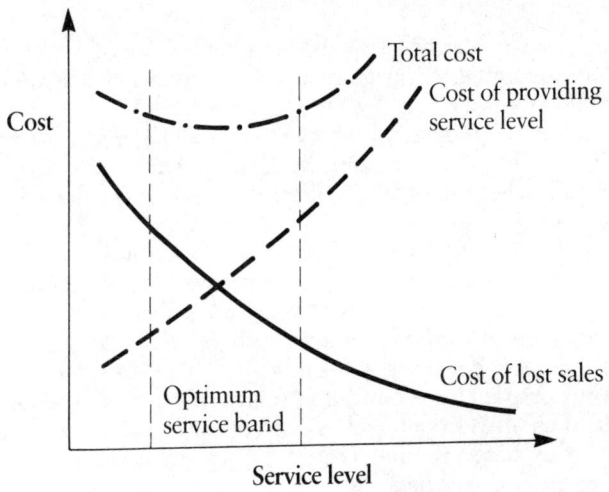

Figure 6   Total distribution cost (TDC) analysis.

of service (Figure 6). The stock levels that need to be carried to support a given level of orders can be calculated fairly easily. Unfortunately order patterns throughout the year may not be even. Adequate stocks for an average month can be inadequate for one month in the year, with the result that customers are lost. A detailed examination of order patterns in previous years will reveal any seasonality in demand for various products and the statistical probability of any peaking of orders.

Stock levels can be defined to provide a theoretical 95% or better probability of being able to meet any demand at any time of year. The company that sells custom-built products may be able to undertake a similar analysis of its component sales.

The stock levels that statistical analyses of historical demand define can be inadequate if demand patterns change or customers react to factors, such as rumours of shortage or imminent price increases, by over ordering. Even here firms have devised approaches that allow them to manage their customers' stocks.

Mars Ltd Confectionery Division in the UK are one company to have operated a consignment stock system. They define the offtake to wholesalers by knowing the latter's stock and by predicting retail demand from historical experience and from their current retail research results. In return for this co-operation the company guarantees to minimize the wholesaler's stock level.

English Sewing, part of the Tootal Group, operate a consignment stock system with their overseas affiliates. The company's main product is thread and while many lines are regular repeat order products, others are subject to the unpredictable demands of fashion.

The company has found that it was better placed to detect sudden changes in demand. To effect control the firm retains ownership of the product in its affiliates' premises and defines the re-order quantities.

Both approaches aim to ease demand management, to minimize the cost of stock holding and to maximize real customer service.

Controlling sudden changes in demand

Very few firms aim to provide 100% ex-stock availability on all products at all times. Ideally the cost of providing various levels of ex-stock availability should be compared with the cost of lost sales which result from being out of stock or being unable to supply within a required lead time. Figure 6 demonstrates the kind of calculation which should be attempted. The total cost line shows a minimum to which the firm should attempt to operate. In practice they will choose a service band.

So far, only the effect of stock level has been cited as a factor which the firm can control to effect service levels and cost levels. In many circumstances the firm should also consider the possibility of varying transport times. Airfreight for example is normally a more expensive mode than surface freight but it can be cheaper if using airfreight allows the seller to reduce stock-holding levels.

One firm manufacturing ladies' gowns was concerned about the lack of larger premises in the centre of the fashion trade of one city. Their manufacturing and main warehousing centre was in another city and the stock area in the first centre was proving inadequate. As their business expanded the showroom also became far too cramped. Rather than continue their search for larger and more expensive premises the firm eventually decided to do away with most of the stockroom in their too small premises, convert these to a larger showroom and rely on the stock held in the manufacturing and main warehousing. By switching their freight mode from surface to air they were able to supply orders placed in the morning by the afternoon with no loss of customer satisfaction. Overall they became more profitable and increased their turnover because of the improvement in display area.

Trading transport costs and speed

Alternative freight modes have to be considered in any review of total distribution costs as well as stock levels but the interaction of both can be equally important. At one extreme all markets can be served from one centre using the fastest freight services. At the other extreme, slower, cheaper freight modes can be used operating from a multitude of secondary warehouses served from central warehousing.

The relative decline in airfreight rates in the 1970s made the former solution more viable. The steady escalation of fuel prices towards the end of that decade and the worldwide recession that deepened during the next decade produced a rise in air rates. As liquid fuel declines in availability and increases in price, some commentators point to an increased potential for rail freight. A distribution system based on rail looks very different from one based on airfreight!

A change in mode can be effected quickly but a change in warehousing structure can take much longer.

Each alternative system has an associated total distribution cost (TDC).

$$TDC = SC + PC + FW + VW + LS$$

where SC = Shipping cost; PC = Packaging cost; FW = Fixed warehousing costs; VW = Variable warehousing costs; LS = Cost of lost sales.

Much depends on the cost of capital the company has to bear. Increased stock levels, warehousing, manning levels all require capital to fund the increased cost. As interest rates rise so this cost increases and the advantage of moving to a faster mode also increases.

Neil Tools, a leading UK manufacturer of hand tools, undertook a total distribution cost analysis of their distribution to North America with the help of the Distribution Advisory Service of British Airways. As a consequence they changed their freight mode from sea and land to air. One of the lines to benefit, singled out by the company, was a relatively expensive tool, a reference vernier. Their American outlets had not been keen to stock such a premium priced line and customers were unwilling to buy with a lead time of twenty-one days. Switching to air reduced the lead time to five days and resulted in sales being made.

Airfreight resulting in a sale

The Neil tools example (above) brings out one further complication for the manufacturer conducting a TDC analysis. Unless the company's goods are fairly similar (homogeneous) in price, profit margin, and weight/volume ratio, a TDC analysis will be quite different for different products. The analysis for all goods might well be different for different geographical markets. Ideally the analysis should be conducted for all products for each market. However firms may be reluctant to have half their supplies travelling by one mode and half by another, half direct and half via warehousing, because of the confusion this could cause, and an average view needs to be taken.

Rather than conduct a long series of analyses it is preferable to estimate the magnitude of any variation from a limited number of analyses and only conduct a complete analysis should the amount of variability prove unacceptable. The more sensitive factors need to be varied to see if unexpected variations in their value would reverse the result of the analysis. Two factors which should be tested in this way are freight rates and the cost of capital.

Channels of distribution

The distribution channel is the term used to refer to the organization structure which a company uses to sell, whole-sale or retail their goods. There is no ideal channel for any particular good. Two of the leading brands of perfumery prove that: Revlon via department stores, chemists and using special instore promotions and Avon selling direct to the public via a large number of part-time agents. Decisions on distribution channels and physical distribution systems over-lap. Parcel post might for example be relevant to Avon and irrelevant to Revlon.

In the international context the exporter has to consider both the national distribution of his product within the overseas market and the distribution of that product to the market itself. Sometimes these are combined, in the case of an exporter of custom built products selling direct to a limited number of customers worldwide. Even here a decision has to be made on the holding of spare parts. Does the idea of holding these in the domestic base offer an adequate service to the customer or should local stocks be made available?

The typical shipping manager or freight forwarder can expect little say in the decision whether to appoint local agents, sell direct, establish an overseas subsidiary or to adopt some other way of serving a new market. Yet his expertise should be of great value in making such decisions and he should be part of the planning process before a company commits itself, perhaps to an agency which it later finds it cannot break, when it discovers a better way of serving the market.

Conversely logistics decisions cannot dominate the channel decision. Legal systems vary so much from one country to another. A simple decision to locate a new warehouse in northern Italy for example to serve central Europe may be correct on location but incorrect due to Italy's tax laws which mitigate against total import and in favour of at least partial local manufacture.

Exporting Completely Knocked Down (CKD) or semi-finished goods to the same location may be the kind of joint decision that logistics, marketing and legal specialists could make together.

A vital decision is how to control the overseas stock levels. The examples on p. 26 identify one approach, the exporter via agreement, or ownership of the stock, is responsible. One problem is that the exporter may have to fund the stockholding.

Because of the credit facilities available, often from governments to encourage exports, the exporter may have few cash problems in owning the overseas stock. For the same reason the overseas agent or subsidiary may not be reluctant to hold stock and consequently be able to provide better customer service. The company may also decide that its own subsidiary is a better choice than a local agent because of the better control which is possible over customer service levels. For the larger company, the true multinational, the choices become greater but more complex.

A leading manufacturer of pharmaceuticals with its base in the USA had manufacturing plant in many countries and sales and marketing outlets in most. The company maintained the flexibility to supply similar products from more than one manufacturing plant. The advantages to them included the taxation benefits of local manufacture but also to have more than one supplier from within their own organization.

As a consequence there was considerable 'cross trading' between different companies in the same group. Rather than leave this to a number of *ad hoc* arrangements, the British subsidiary was given responsibility for the co-ordination of the distribution of cross-traded goods.

Multiple sourcing within the same multinational

The multinational can evolve a complex pattern of channels of distribution and physical distribution systems as illustrated by the example (above). The question then arises, how can a company be confident that such a pattern is both operating well and indeed that a totally different pattern should not be implemented?

The distribution audit

The term 'distribution audit' has come to be used to refer to a very broad but very detailed analysis of a company's entire distribution process including both channel and physical distribution. The easiest way of describing the process is to draw the analogy with the more familiar accounting audit.

Here the assets and liabilities of the firm are assessed together with its record of what has been achieved in the last twelve months. It is a statement that every limited company must obtain (from in this case an independent auditor) that the position of the firm is fairly stated in its annual accounts. To make this statement the external auditors delve into the minutae of the firm's business assessing all the financial records and processes.

In the same way the distribution auditor assesses every aspect of the (probably his own) firm's methods of delivering goods via the distribution channel to their customers. Various attempts have been made to offer the domestic practitioner a list of questions to ask or tables to complete. There is unfortunately no version known to the author that approaches the problems peculiar to international distribution, although the various national approaches could well be adapted. Given the range of products, markets and stages of international development from one firm to another, it is doubtful whether one set of questions or pro formas would prove adequate for even the majority of companies.

There are nevertheless a number of guidelines which could provide the basis for any company seeking to analyse their distribution processes.

1　Availability of data: Is cost information available or can it be estimated for every link in the distribution process for each type of product? (Frankly, if it is not, forget about a distribution audit until the data base can be established!)

2 Which costs/revenues are the largest and/or the most variable?

3 What changes have occurred over the last year? (This will identify those areas which could be examined in greater detail at the start of the audit.)

4 What alternative systems are available? (These will identify alternatives for investigation which could be more cost effective than the system being used.)

A very limited example will show both the potential of the distribution audit for analysis, decision making and for generating a great deal of work before any decision can be taken!

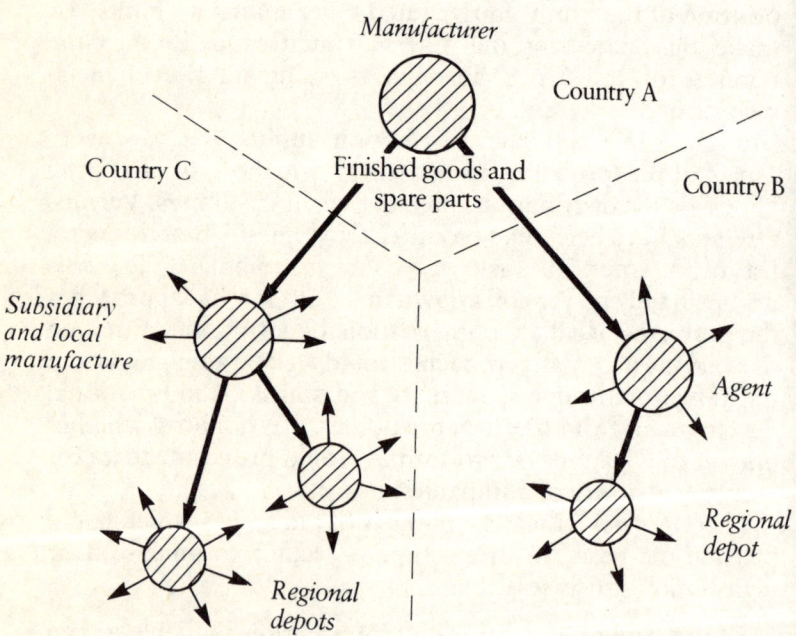

Figure 7   The distribution audit.

Figure 7 shows, schematically, a manufacturer in Country A exporting finished goods and spare parts to an agent in Country B (terms of sale 90 days in sterling, terms of trade CIF) and to subsidiary in Country C who do some manufacturing from components sent from Country A (terms of sale 30 days in sterling, terms of trade ex-works).

Country B sells and distributes from the main office and from a regional depot, Country C from the main office and two regional depots.

A comparison between Markets B and C showed roughly equal sales volumes but Market C had a much lower profit on sales. Selling prices in both countries were both towards the top end of the market. Potentially Country C, as a subsidiary, should have been more profitable than Country B, served by an agent who was also making his profit.

An examination of all the costs involved showed that international freight paid was higher to Country C. The terms of transfer pricing were changed to take advantage of the apparently more effective purchasing of freight in headquarters.

The main overheads in Country C were found to be the costs of warehousing. The regional depots were offering excellent service but at a high cost. A TDC analysis indicated that the buffer stocks held at the main office in Country C could be reduced if a more expensive, but faster, means of freight were used. This would also release rented warehousing.

Another analysis showed that the local manufacturing capacity in Country C was being under-used while Country A management was paying overtime rates to keep pace with assembly for Country B. Country B was thereafter partially sourced from Country C.

All these changes may appear logical and straightforward. Deciding that these are the changes to be made involves considerable effort which can involve calling on help from other line functions in the firm. However it is only by undertaking such an exercise that such changes can be made on the basis of objective data, used to make an analytical decision, rather than by having to resort to judgement made on the basis of limited, and perhaps faulty, information.

Keypoints

1 In any business certain tasks exist: the responsibility for these is divided between various line functions.
2 A number of management concepts have evolved to encourage the co-ordination of the often fragmented responsibility for the many aspects of distribution.
3 Physical Distribution Management (PDM) emphasizes that the various components in distribution need to be seen as one combined cost.
4 Materials management is concerned with optimizing the distribution system at the input end of the firm.
5 The logistics concept combines the two ideas of PDM and materials management. It is the task of moving goods into and through the firm and on to the customer and the movement of information in the reverse direction.
6 International logistics, in the context of this text, is concerned with the efficient movement of the export order through the firm and to the customer.
7 Total distribution cost (TDC) analysis is the calculation that allows the balancing of distribution and service costs with the price of failing to serve the customer.
8 The distribution audit is a comprehensive review of how a firm gets its goods to the customer.

References and further reading

1 SHYCON, H. N. and SPRAGUE, C. R., 'Put a Price tag on your customer servicing levels' *Harvard Business Review*, July/August, 1975.
2 Mentioned in 'Logistics in a Marketing Context' Christopher, M. *Eur. J. Marketing*, Vol. 6, 2, 1972, p. 117.

SLIGPER, MARTIN *Distribution for Exporters* British Institute of Management Guide, No. 6, 1977.
BREAM, ROLAND and WILSON SMITH, JOHN *Distribution Audit Workbook* (Centre for Physical Distribution Management, London, 1978).
BOWERSOX, DONALD J. *Logistical Management* (Collier, 1980).

PART TWO
The management of international distribution

3
Organizational choices for the manufacturer

It is always difficult to find two companies organized in exactly the same way. It is particularly difficult to find two companies organized in the same way for international distribution because of the wide range of choice open to them. Nevertheless the choices they have fall into only two broad areas: the relationships they form with external organizations, notably freight forwarders; and the position of the shipping function within the firm.

External choices

Exporters and importers need not involve themselves in any way with the details of distribution and documentation. The freight forwarder (*see* Chapter 13) can act as the shipper's agent in purchasing freight services, selecting route and mode and in preparing all necessary documentation. He is both an agent and an adviser. The role of the traditional forwarder who is unassociated with any one transport or carrier company has declined in favour of the secondary carrier function. Nevertheless secondary carriers, and carriers themselves, undertake forwarding functions. The choice for the shipper is between how much use does he make of these bought-in services and how much is conducted in-house.

Figure 8 demonstrates the three options open for the shipper. Organizationally international distribution can be represented by three boxes laid side by side representing three links in a chain, the exporter, the forwarder and the carrier.

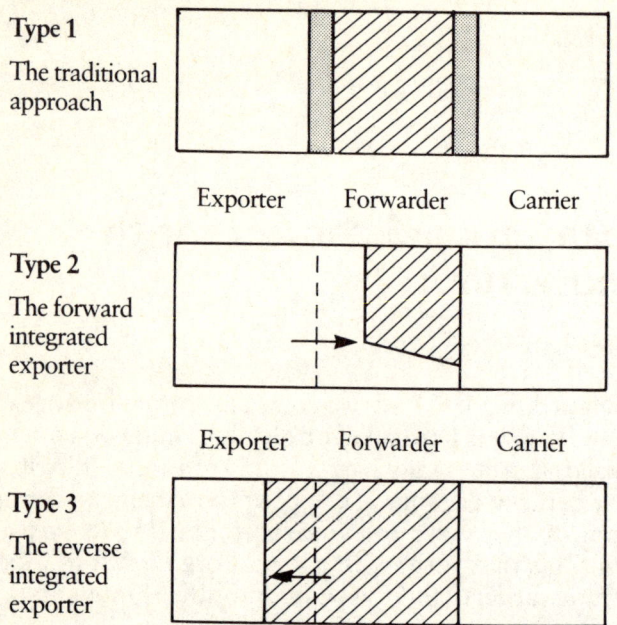

Figure 8   The three types of relationship between exporter and forwarder.

The traditional approach

In the traditional approach the shipper relies exclusively on one or more forwarders to undertake his shipping and documentation. The company may justify their choice by claiming that 'their business is manufacturing and sales – not distribution' or that 'our firm is too small to cope with the complexities of distribution, we leave that to the experts'.

Significantly the forwarder, while he is entrusted with getting the company's goods to their destination on time and at minimum cost, is dealt with at arm's length. There is a definite barrier, a demarcation line, between shipper and forwarder. The forwarder may only know about a new market that his client has recently entered when he receives the first consignment. The lack of integration between what the two are doing makes it difficult and sometimes impossible to

evolve a systematic approach to distribution. The international logistics concepts of easing the movement of the order
through the firm on export and optimizing the flow of
materials into the firm on import demands that there be one
single authority and responsibility in control. In the traditional
approach neither shipper nor forwarder can claim such a role.
It is not enough to argue that both sides 'work closely
together': one or other must have control if a single system is
going to operate.

Years ago, when international trade was dominated by
carriage by sea and transit times were extended, the traditional
approach was adequate. In the modern world, where delivery
times and delivery reliability are key factors, this approach can
be inadequate. Nevertheless this approach is still adopted by
many firms for all their international traffic and by many more
in their dealings with airfreight.

One company, who could be categorized as adopting a
traditional approach to international logistics, manufactured
specialist plant. Three instances illustrate the problems that
can arise when no-one has an overview of all aspects of
logistics.

Incident 1. A large piece of machinery had just been
completed. The shipping line had delivered the container
ordered by the company's freight forwarder and were eager
to load the machinery. Unfortunately a last minute design
change had resulted in a control box being added to the side
of the machine. This meant that the machine would no
longer fit into the container but the consignment had to leave
there and then. The control box was removed with a welding
torch and the machine shipped leaving the customer to
replace the box and repaint the machine.

Incident 2. An even larger piece of machinery was carefully
shipped to America. Because there were no low-loader
lorries available at the docks the machinery proved too tall
to pass beneath the overhead traffic lights in the city.

Incident 3. Because management was concerned about the
risks of bad debts in dealing with certain markets, an

instruction was issued to the effect that no goods were to be despatched to these markets without receiving either cash with order or a letter of credit. A major customer was infuriated by a demand from a clerk for a letter of credit or cash before he would despatch a spare part worth 25 pence.

The problems of a traditional approach

Forward integration

Most companies have replaced at least a part of the traditional forwarder's role by an in-house function. They deal directly with the carrier, they prepare their own export documentation and customs entries or they undertake their own export packing.

Some companies go much further. Large multi-site firms have formed their own consolidation points to avoid paying large numbers of minimum freight charges. Some have set up their own forwarding subsidiaries.

Freight forwarders are still retained but only to serve the minor markets, to deal with the Consular procedures where the company is a long distance from the nearest Consulate, and to deal with airfreight. In some countries forwarders and specialist customs agents have some degree of monopoly over their role: even here there is a trend worldwide for shippers to replace much of the forwarder's traditional role.

There are a number of explanations for this evolutionary process. Unit loading in general and containerization in particular has lessened the need for supervision of cargo at many points in its movement between consignee and consignor. The development of local customs clearance centres away from the coastal docks has made it easier for shippers to oversee their own cargo movements. The physical movement of goods has become easier.

Most country's export efforts are highly concentrated: a minority of firms account for the majority of exports. The larger firms have found it cost effective to acquire their own expertise rather than rely upon the bought-in services of the traditional forwarder. Professionalism has also played its part. Many shipping managers feel with such justification that their role is undervalued. Undertaking more inside the firm of what used to be bought in from outside enlarges their role, which can be presented as being more significant to senior management.

In many instances quite genuine economies can be achieved through an in-house service. This is particularly in documentation where the cost of clerical and bought-in costs is remarkably high (*see* Chapter 5). The advent of aligned documentation has meant that if the company produces its own commercial invoice (and almost all do) it may as well produce a large number of other international documents which it would previously have been the forwarder's role to provide.

The move towards an in-house forwarding function has been paralleled by a move to control other associated services, export packing for example. In Europe many companies undertake part of their own international transportation using their own lorries. The logical product of a larger company moving into forwarding is the evolution of its own forwarding company who offer services to other traders. While it is logical there could be some unexpected consequences, which are discussed later together with the issue of centralization.

There are benefits for the exporter to replace previously bought-in services other than those of cost reduction and professionalism and these are associated with having one organization responsible for the complete movement of goods from consignor to consignee. In these circumstances there is a greater opportunity to introduce the systematic approach which we have called international logistics.

In Chapter 1 the growing importance of trade was emphasized. At the level of the firm many companies have found that ever more of their revenue is from export markets. At the same time the trading pattern of many companies, especially British companies, has become more concentrated. The proportion of UK trade going to and from Western Europe increased dramatically in the late 1970s. With large established sales in a foreign market the firm sets up a subsidiary. It has control at both ends of the transit and it is logical for it to undertake all forwarding activities associated with these major flows of goods.

One major European multinational realized the potential for establishing large component plants in different countries to feed their assembly plants throughout Europe. The company organized a distribution system using its own containers which were routed from one site to another linking all the company's production units.

Multinational control

The potential for forward integration is not in any way restricted to the large company. Many small firms, including import and export agents, can make most of their income from astute management of international distribution. One such company imported 40 ft container loads of textiles from South East Asia into the UK, divided the loads into 20 ft containers for on shipment to West Africa. The ultimate buyer was apparently unaware of the availability of a direct service using the 20 ft containers which were the largest he could handle locally. The small UK company profited from its better knowledge of the admittedly complex international distribution industry.

Profit for small firms by forward integration

Reverse integration

The forwarding community has inevitably responded to the move by exporters to replace them in their role. For many years traders have been able to hire a forwarder's employee as a replacement for having their own shipping manager. The individual also acts as an organizational bridge between exporter and forwarder.

A logical extension of this approach is for the forwarding company to replace much if not all of the exporter's traditional shipping department with its own organization either physically inside or outside of the client company. The problem for the client is that should things go awry and the forwarding concern prove incompetent it is no easy task to replace them.

The advantages to the company include the same benefits that accrue to the forward integrated importer or exporter — one organization is responsible for all or most of the logistics role. Small- and medium-sized companies could be particularly attracted to the second of the integrated approaches but the idea has been adopted by large firms and conglomerates of small firms as well.

One major exporter consolidated all of its export sales of components on to one site. Previously, different companies in the group had each served export markets independently. When the new organization was formed it became obvious that there were too many freight and forwarding companies serving the organization. It was not unusual for a queue of collect and delivery vehicles to form outside the company's premises. Part of the problem concerned the company's own export terms of sale which were FOB. This gave the consignee the right to nominate the freight company. As the terms of sale in the industry were also FOB the company were reluctant to change to delivered pricing. The other part of the problem was that individual shipping managers from the companies forming the new centralized unit each had their own preference in freight firms. The company eventually standardized on only one freight forwarder who was also an international carrier. Each day the forwarder provided one trailer for all consignments. These were taken to the forwarder's own premises for on-shipment. The company modified its terms of sale to FOB plus services. Customers were not strictly obliged to use the new system but any requests to do otherwise were rigorously investigated. If the customer could demonstrate that he had found a better way of transporting the goods, the exporter's forwarder was instructed to change his procedures. Alternatively the customer was still free to arrange to pick up goods but from the exporter's forwarder and at extra expense. Normally the exporter and his forwarder arranged freight, technically as the agent of the consignee who was invoiced for the FOB value of the goods plus freight charges.

Both exporter and forwarder saved considerable clerical costs by agreeing a fee based, not on the number of items processed or the work involved in each but, on the export value of the goods handled. This percentage covered all services up to FOB and had been calculated by totalling previous year's fees. However the real value to the firm, and any customer, was that a system had been installed to ease the flow of goods from one to another.

A large exporter in reverse integration

A major exporter exported primarily to fellow subsidiaries in a multinational pharmaceutical company. Terms of sale for inter-company transfers were ex-works. Each unit acted as a separate profit centre. The UK company accepted a proposal from its shipping manager to set up a separate company to handle both their export forwarding and export order processing. The cost of both was moved outside the firm and then became the responsibility of the consignee. The new company offered a similar service to other firms who were attracted to use it because of the cost savings from using the export administration company's knowledge as a forwarding company and the use of their computerized order processing and documentation system which would reduce their order processing costs. The computer system was applicable mainly to high repeat order products and proved difficult to market, probably because a major cost saving for clients was the cost of their own shipping department which would now be redundant.

Financial advantages in reverse integration

Which approach?

The nature of the changes in international trade have encouraged a move away from the traditional approach to one of the two integrated approaches. Most companies have chosen forward integration but either integrated approach has the potential for the evolution of a more systematic approach to distribution which will reduce costs and improve customer service. Apart from having to rely upon a bought-in service the third approach has the disadvantage associated with relying upon one service company should anything happen to that company. On the other hand the bought-in service can be attractive to a company with a seasonal export trade.

The traditional approach is forced upon some companies because of the nature of their custom-built products. Most firms have this approach in airfreight because of the dominance of the airfreight forwarder in that market although some have moved towards reverse integration in airfreight with one chosen forwarder by putting one of their own employees into the air forwarding firm to oversee their freight movements.

Centralization

The advantages of centralizing a business function in a multisite company are usually given as economies of scale and the ability to employ specialist management. To these must be added increased purchasing power in the case of international logistics.

Typical figures for a developed country on the concentration of export effort are that 85% of export volume is generated by 15% of exporters. These statistics imply that an exporter acts as a single corporate body when exporting. The reality is that most conglomerates are highly decentralized for their sales, marketing and distribution. Indeed within any one exporting unit it is not unknown to find a number of shipping managers or clerks working separately, each shipping similar goods (from a distribution perspective) to identical markets using different carriers. While there are some advantages in the flexibility of complete decentralization with an individual shipping clerk allocated to each product group, most companies opt for some degree of centralization.

The first stage in centralization is the formation of an identifiable shipping department. In Chapter 4 the often part-time nature of the shipping function is discussed. This is typical of the 'traditional' organization approach, if the major part of the function is bought in there is no reason to have a separate, specialist shipping department. The department, once established, can grow in one of two ways, either it takes on more of the traditionally bought-in services or its work load expands because of increased export sales over time.

This process can be demonstrated by plotting the notional level of involvement of the firm in forwarding activities over time, assuming that the firm's trading volumes increase with time (Figure 9).

Typically the firm evolves from its traditional structure towards a greater involvement in forwarding in a series of steps. It begins negotiating directly with carriers, it undertakes its own documentation, and so on. At a certain stage in a large firm the previously separate shipping functions are central-ized. The central department can undertake all of the shipping and forwarding work for the firm's peripheral units or act as an advisory body with perhaps a central negotiating role.

The temptation is to evolve a highly centralized department perhaps located at corporate headquarters which acts as the only shipping function in the firm. In the early stages of its existence the idea can work well. The increased negotiating power of the central unit means cheaper freight rates and better service from carriers. The centralization of expertise means the company can afford to spend time on developing new clerical systems, computer systems and money on route and mode research. At this stage the central service must be used by all operating units. It is funded perhaps by a levy on all freight purchased or as a central service adding to the overheads of operating units: in other words as a cost centre in the firm.

Two pressures result in the central service becoming a separate profit centre in the group offering its services on a

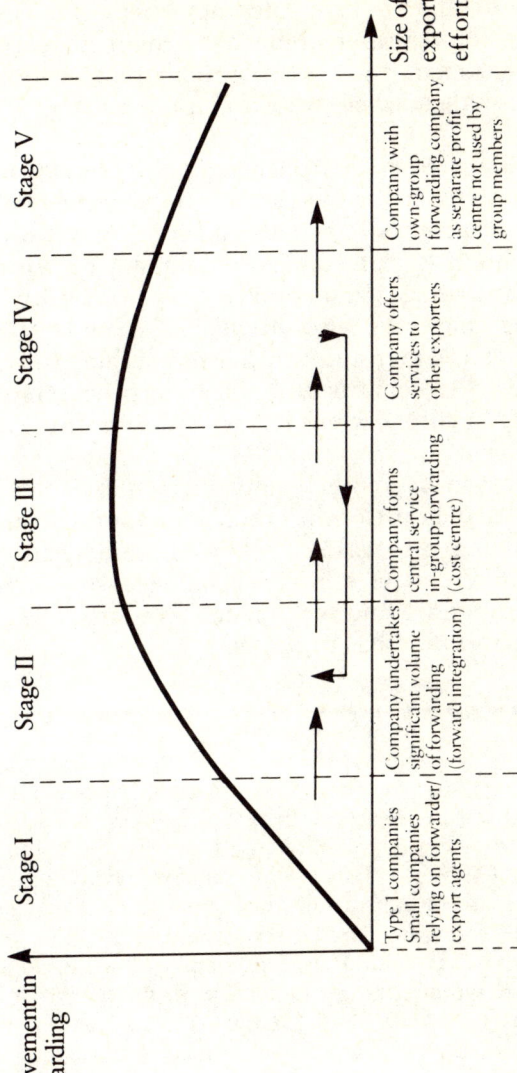

Figure 9 A life-cycle model of an exporter's involvement in forwarding.

commercial basis to both group members and outsiders. Individual units in the group begin to find fault with the central service. It is too far away. The rates they offer can be bettered locally. Furthermore the senior management in the centralized shipping department realize the potential of selling their services to smaller firms who cannot afford their own expertise.

The central service moves from being a cost centre to being a profit centre, offering its services both to group members and to outsiders on a commercial basis and competing with other forwarding concerns. At this stage the company's involvement in its own forwarding is at its peak. The in-house forwarding and shipping unit may also become a secondary carrier subcontracting its own transport, chartering ships and leasing containers. The new unit is well placed to offer competitive rates to the destinations which its own major traffic flows are moving between.

For one reason or another individual units in the group begin to reduce their use of the group's forwarding company. When evaluating the reasons behind such a change it is difficult to differentiate between genuine cost and service reasons for any move and the inevitable politics with which any large organization has to contend.

One large multisite exporter had a central shipping department offering services to group companies scattered throughout the UK. One of the companies in the group who declined to use their services was perhaps the closest geographically to the central unit. One reason they gave was that they had found that they could load containers with their product more efficiently than the central unit. To the outside observer there is an anomaly in this assertion. If the one company had developed a better system would it not be preferable for the central unit to acquire this knowledge and for the manufacturing unit to retain the advantages of dealing with the central service?

Politics and centralization

Having broken with the central forwarding function, individual firms within the group have now only limited expertise within their own organizations and still rely heavily on freight forwarders, albeit one or more of their own choice. The overall involvement of the firm in its own forwarding declines but this does not mean that the in-house forwarding company fails. It is usual in fact for both exporting units and forwarder to continue to prosper. The problem is that individual firms have to begin to evolve a single system to oversee their own freight.

In an effort to counter the decline in own company usage of the central service once it becomes a separate profit centre some companies insist that the in-house forwarding or transport concern must be given the opportunity to quote for any group company business.

The large multisite company seems to go through a life-cycle in its involvement in forwarding. The involvement grows until shipping is centralized. Then it declines as the central service becomes, in effect, similar to any other forwarding company as far as the operating units are concerned.

Levels of centralization

Large firms can choose to centralize completely or decentralize completely. There are a number of intermediate choices which have proved relatively successful.

One of the UK's largest companies was organized into operating divisions. Each division had a number of manufacturing plants and the distribution function was centralized at divisional level. In addition a separate head office function was responsible for the consolidation of small consignments moving from different divisions to the same destination. This function retained offices at the major ports, negotiated some freight contracts centrally and appointed a single airfreight forwarder to deal with all group airfreight.

Partial centralization

A highly diverse company retained a central shipping department based on one of its largest manufacturing units. It was then both the shipping department for that unit and the central department for the group. It was funded partially by a levy on all freight purchases made by individual group companies. The idea was that in many circumstances the purchasing power of the central unit would provide freight rates below those obtained by group companies. Despite this, and the levy, companies frequently made their own arrangements.

Non-use of a centralized function

A major American multinational vehicle and components manufacturer believed in the merits of a decentralized divisional structure. In 1977 they created a central, international logistics department focusing upon transportation, packaging and freight handling. Their challenge was to achieve the benefits of a co-ordinated corporate approach without losing the advantages of divisional focus on local considerations. The function concentrated on consolidating divisional freight movements and the elimination of the duplication of effort.

While the divisional emphasis was seen as operational, corporate staff were concerned with a forward planning and research function. New and creative solutions were identified to anticipated and existing problems.

The concentration of expertise allowed the development of sophisticated analytical and modelling tools to aid in the forecasting of vessel availability, shifts in demand patterns and sourcing volumes and locations.

The central service served as a management resource, developing systems for individual divisions. It also helped reduce costs directly by negotiating a corporate-forwarder agreement.

Source: International Logistics Management at General Motors: Philosophy and Practice; R. E. Krapfel, J. T. Mentzer, R. R. Williams, *Int. J. Physical Distribution and Materials Management*, Vol. 11, No. 5/6, 1981, p. 12–20.

The role of a head office function

The practical experience of a number of large organizations implies that whatever the theoretical advantages for total centralization of international logistics management, in practice complete centralization brings only temporary benefits to individual companies. Some measure of centralization can be beneficial when operating units do not see the central service as a threat to their autonomy.

Companies who do choose to centralize fully will probably face the inevitable separation of the central service as a new company, which may be no bad thing given the historical expansion of international trade.

Where in the organization?

A highly centralized shipping/forwarding department could well report directly to main board level. Most companies do not seem to opt for this approach and are faced with one more major organizational choice: with which line function, if any, to associate the shipping function?

In a survey of UK shipping managers[1] the following reporting relationships predominated:

Export	15%
Sales/marketing	9%
Commercial services	11%
Company Secretary/finance	13%
Distribution	9%

The remainder (over 40%) could not be allocated to any of these categories and had a very wide range of reporting relationships.

The results of the survey reflect a long-running debate on the relative merits of marketing, finance and distribution as the ultimate reporting relationship and the apparent lack of any one obvious choice.

In part the choice will be constrained by the firm's products. A large custom-built product will tend to be managed by project team and one member of that team will have the responsibility for shipping. To whom he reports within the team or within the firm is likely to be less important than his ability to act as a member of that team.

The marketing claim

Good communication and a good understanding between shipping and export sales is important. Combining the two functions can provide this advantage. However if sales become over-concerned with customer service and become over-eager to despatch part orders by expensive freight modes there can be certain disbenefits in increased cost.

Conceptually logistics management is certainly concerned with customer service and if the export, sales, and marketing figures cited above are totalled then the most frequently used reporting relationship in the UK is to marketing. Figure 10 outlines the typical organization in a medium-sized company who have adopted this approach.

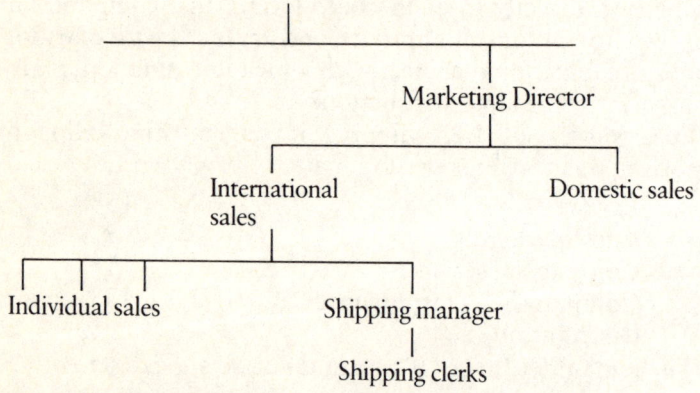

Figure 10   Organization chart for medium-sized company with shipping reporting to marketing.

The distribution claim

Many managers view international distribution as merely more complex than national distribution and argue for a combined organizational structure. If this argument is true similar skills are required for each aspect and a combined approach will allow a greater concentration of management expertise.

However export order sizes, especially for high repeat order products, are usually much higher than domestic order sizes. In domestic trade the major management skill is in the efficient handling of large numbers of small consignments rather than the efficient handling of the complex order processing associated with export. Nevertheless both distribution tasks share the same problems of order picking and packing, warehousing, and transport buying. Figure 11 outlines one organizational structure used by a large company who had adopted this approach. Their administration is quite complex. The synergy claimed for combining the two distribution functions is sometimes impossible to achieve.

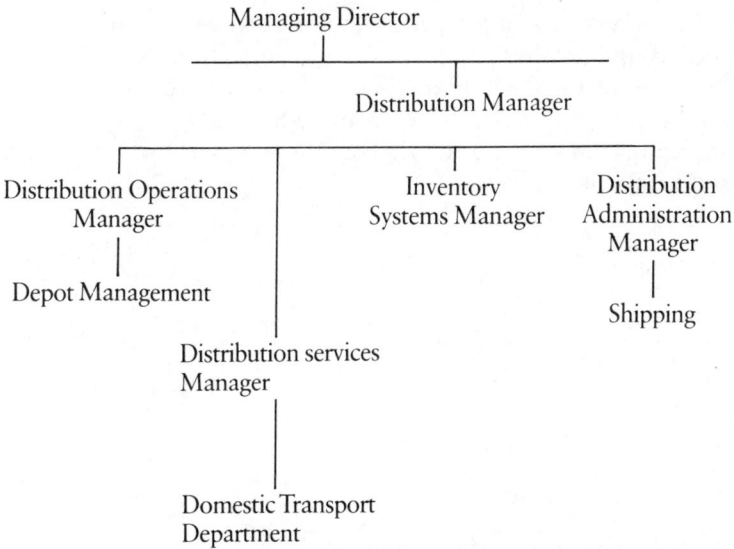

Figure 11 Organization chart for one large company with shipping associated with domestic distribution.

The finance claim

Trading procedures, especially with less developed markets and with Comecon countries, are often complex. The use of letters of credit and bills of exchange in international trade while facilitating trade with difficult markets means there is little room for error. In dealing with deep sea markets a key transportation document, the bill of lading, is also a key commercial document in that it is a document of title and a proof of despatch. As the latter, it allows the exporter to discount a bill of exchange with his bank.

The inter-relationship of finance and distribution is the basic argument for combining the two roles. Under British law every limited company must have a Company Secretary. The position has a range of legal responsibilities. In some firms the role is built upon to establish a combined legal and financial responsibility which can include the detailed negotiation of contracts.

In other firms order processing is seen as a financial task providing another reason for placing shipping within a financial framework. Figure 12 outlines the organization of a medium-sized engineering firm who chose to associate shipping with the Company Secretary role within a broader financial role.

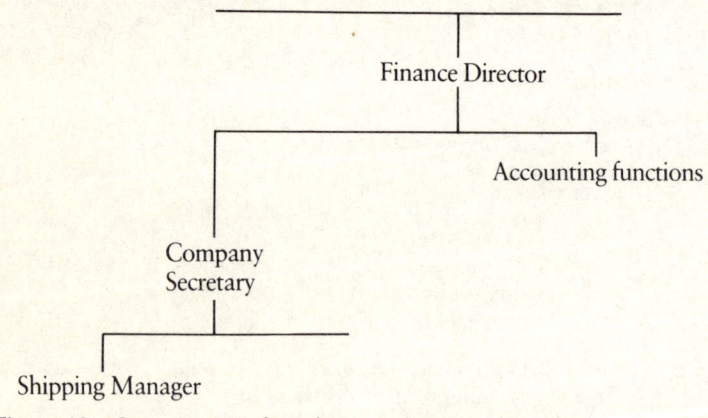

Figure 12   Organization chart for a medium-sized engineering firm with shipping within finance.

The commercial services claim

Firms are sometimes criticized for creating a commercial services division to contain all the functions which cannot be fitted anywhere else in the organization. Nevertheless there is an argument for treating shipping as a service function in the firm and giving it a certain amount of independence by *not* placing it within distribution, finance or marketing.

A centralized shipping department is also likely to be part of a central services unit.

One firm evolved a purchasing and distribution function (Figure 13) as one example of a central services organization. A closer examination of the approach indicates that there is potential to evolve a logistics function on the lines of the domestic logistics concept where the flow of goods through the firm is a well-defined task. In practice such a system was not formally applied, the organization being one of administrative convenience rather than being deliberately designed to ease the flow of goods from purchasing through warehousing and on to the customer via distribution.

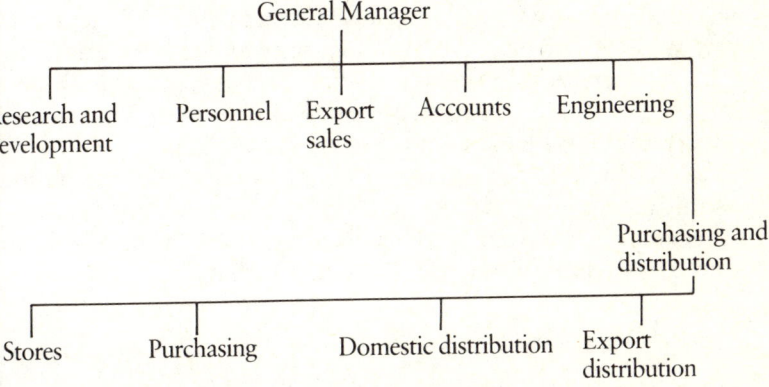

Figure 13　Organization chart with shipping associated with other service functions.

Other claims

The specific problems posed by the nature of an individual firm's goods have already been mentioned as a factor in determining reporting relationships. Other pragmatic factors can dominate the decision. One writer even went so far as to suggest that the very arguments used by different line functions to control the shipping function made it tempting to divide shipping into its constituent parts and allocate the tasks throughout the firm, order acknowledgement to sales, order processing to accounts, freight purchasing to buying, and so on.

All the examples cited so far have been drawn from British or American companies. The approaches which seem to dominate German and French companies are somewhat different. In French firms it is usual to see the company organized around a domestic market which consists of France and all other EEC countries. Other markets, or *le grand marché*, are dealt with separately. There is a definite logic behind this, if the EEC is to become a truly domestic market and since France is a country so centrally placed in the Community.

In German firms it is unusual to find an export distribution specialist. The shipping manager does not seem to be a widely accepted role. Instead the typical German firm will tend to have a highly integrated marketing, sales and export administration function with the day-to-day tasks associated with the shipping manager dealt with by a junior member of the department who liaises with outside forwarders.

With the relative success of France and Germany as exporting nations these two points cannot be ignored, especially the propensity towards integration in the German firm and within a marketing function at that.

Which option?

There is no clearly identifiable ideal reporting relationship for the shipping function. However, if the reader accepts the argument of the need for a logistics approach, whatever solution is adopted should be compatible with the concept of easing the export order through the firm. This implies that the marketing/sales claim is the most logical and the German experience would support this to an extent.

Sales or marketing should be involved in order processing at least initially, because they need to know what effect their efforts are having in the market place. The problems that can be caused by an over-ambitious delivery promise have been mentioned earlier. Better communication between sales and shipping promoted by integrating the two functions is one solution. Sales need to be involved in order processing, as well as shipping, who need to prepare the complex export documentation. Establishing one system to ease the movement of the order through the firm makes it doubly logical to combine the two functions.

There is an alternative which can produce the same effect, especially in the firm exporting mainly to its own subsidiaries where the sales' emphasis is in the consignee's country. This is for the presence of a strong shipping function able to speak to other parts of the company at senior management level. Where this function is located is less relevant than that the authority is given to institute a systematic approach to export logistics. Whereas the marketing/sales choice does not require a top quality manager to be responsible for shipping, especially if the company tend to sell ex-works, the alternative approach requires a high calibre individual to ensure that a system can be implemented and maintained.

Import logistics

Much of what has been said about the claims of marketing to export logistics can be applied to the import side for both purchasing and production planning. Again if the reader accepts the import logistics concept outlined in Chapter 2 the claims of either function can be argued as similar to marketing on export. Either import needs to be integrated into the function responsible for the smooth supply of materials into the business or it must be managed by an individual strong enough to impose the necessary informal system.

On occasion a company has sufficient import and export traffic to raise the issue of whether it is desirable to integrate both tasks. The arguments presented in this chapter imply that unless the two have some commonality of interest (for example in the smooth movement of goods between subsidiaries on a regular basis) then the two tasks are somewhat dissimilar and should be maintained separately.

Keypoints

1 Organizational choices can be divided into three types: the relationship with external companies especially freight forwarders; the level of centralization; and the reporting relationships within a company.
2 Companies are moving away from a traditional to one of two evolved forms of relationship with freight forwarders, either of which enable a logistics system to be established.
3 Centralization contains mixed blessings. Apparently, inevitably, a centralized service becomes a separate profit centre outside the organization.
4 Some degree of centralization is applied by most large companies
5 Many line functions can lay claim to the shipping function. The claims of marketing and sales are often the most valid on export and purchasing or production scheduling on import. The alternative is for the head of shipping to be sufficiently powerful in the firm to ensure the maintenance of a logistics approach.

References and further reading

1 DAVIES, G. J. and GRAY, R. *Who Buys International Freight Services* (Maclean Hunter, London, 1980).

DAVIES, G. J. 'The Role of Exporter and Freight Forwarder in the United Kingdom'. *J. Int. Bus. Studies*, Winter, 1981, p. 99.

4
The role of the international logistics manager

Precisely what any one manager does on a day-to-day basis for the organization in which he works varies greatly according to the type of product produced and the size of the company concerned. The international logistics manager's role (or that of shipping manager as he is likely to be called at least in the United Kingdom) is no exception. Nevertheless it is useful to examine the kind of tasks which practising managers undertake, especially as the span of control of the shipping manager is very wide.

A typical export order would proceed through a number of

Enquiry from customer
Quotation
Receipt of order
Credit rating check
Order acknowledgement
  and delivery promise
Order produced
Order assembled
Order packed
Invoice produced
Export documentation produced
Transport procured
Despatch
Credit control

Figure 14   The main stages in the export order process.

stages, identified in Figure 14, and it would not be unusual for a shipping department to be responsible for all but the production process, not unusual that is if the company has shipping associated with export sales. When the two are divided sales tends to handle everything until the order is ready for despatch when the shipping department is largely concerned with preparing the necessary documentation (only the export invoice if the company relies heavily on an outside forwarder) and with purchasing the necessary transport and associated forwarding services.

As well as the routine support of the order process the shipping manager should also be concerned with influencing other areas in the firm whose actions, or the lack of them, impinge upon both his area of direct responsibility and the wider mission of international logistics.

Within the shipping department, whatever its responsibilities, the different tasks are dealt with at different levels in the hierarchy. Mode choice, for example, between surface and airfreight, could well be a decision requiring the attention of the shipping manager and his superior while the choice of

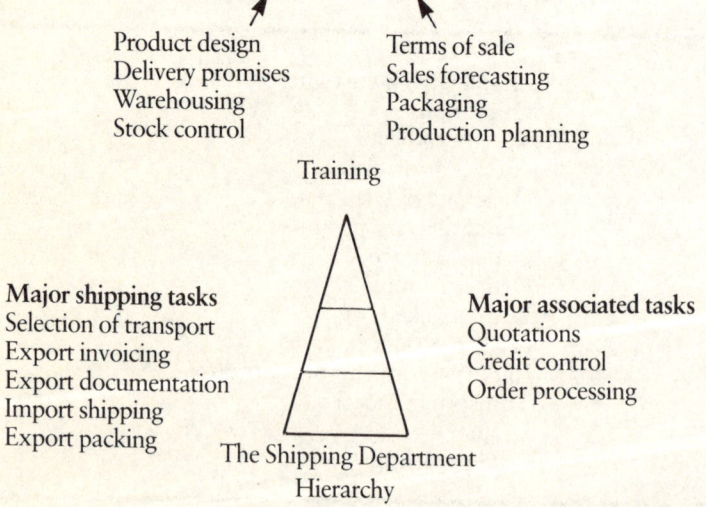

Main areas for influence

Product design   Terms of sale
Delivery promises   Sales forecasting
Warehousing   Packaging
Stock control   Production planning

Training

Major shipping tasks   **Major associated tasks**
Selection of transport   Quotations
Export invoicing   Credit control
Export documentation   Order processing
Import shipping
Export packing

The Shipping Department
Hierarchy

Figure 15   Tasks associated with export logistics.

operator within a mode could be the shipping manager's and the selection of one out of a list of approved operators, a task delegated to a junior level.

Figure 15 represents the previous paragraphs diagrammatically. A distinction is made between the essential tasks associated with export shipping, those tasks which are closely associated with the role and which may form a part of a wider role in combination with sales, and those areas the role should seek to influence and liaise with to meet the wider logistics concept.

Import shipping would be much more closely associated with production planning and purchasing as major associated tasks.

Internal organization

In some companies the shipping department consists of perhaps one or two people. In the smaller firms such individuals will frequently be responsible for other export-related activities outside order processing and transportation.

As the number of export consignments increases so does the number of people required to undertake the shipping task until the point is reached where the department is large enough to merit a decision between a horizontal and vertical organization.

In the vertical approach the separate tasks in the department are performed by specialists in that task. In the horizontal approach all tasks to one market or for one product type are conducted by one individual, a specialist in that market or product field.

It is argued that the vertical approach develops greater expertise, but the job satisfaction of dealing day in, day out with letters of credit for example, can be questioned. Rotating individual responsibilities, irrespective of the approach adopted, merits consideration.

Dealing with other functions

One of the consequences of ascribing a low status to international distribution in the firm is that other functions in the firm find it easier to ignore the necessity of considering the interaction of their role with the demands of cost effective distribution and optimum customer service. International logistics managers must seek to identify a number of aspects in other management areas where their expertise can contribute to the goals of the firm.

Product design

Changes in dimensions can dramatically affect packing densities in unit load devices. A move towards completely knocked down (ckd) manufacturing can be cost effective where freight costs are high. Distant markets with one climate are often reached via areas with very different climates. The resilience of delicate products can be tested severely when carried over unmade roads or transhipped by inexperienced labour in developing countries.

Marketing

The buyer may be better served by changing the company's terms of sale to offer a delivered price if the exporter can procure freight at advantageous rates. Changing the unit of sale to match the capacity of a unit load device, especially the ISO container, can save greatly on shipping costs. Shipping parts of the completed product separately can mean declaring components under different tariff headings, attracting lower shipping charges, and lower tariffs.

Production planning

Many export orders can only be considered as firm orders when a letter of credit is received. However the experience of dealing with the customer or the market in the past can enable production planning to take a view on the advantages of producing to the order before confirmation. All too often an export order can be lost if, when the letter of credit arrives, there is too little time to meet the required delivery date. In any case liaison with production planning should be a vital area, as producing the right goods, at the right time, is an essential part of maintaining customer service while minimizing the cost of inventory.

Stock control

A total distribution cost analysis is one method of optimizing stock levels. The more efficient the company's delivery system, the lower their stocks and, more importantly, those of their subsidiaries, distributors and customers need be.

Warehousing

One of the warehousing tasks is to mark packed goods ready for shipment. Close liaison between warehousing and shipping is an obvious objective where case markings have to concur with a letter of credit and be in a foreign language. Just as important is the need to minimize packing and picking errors in order assembly. Errors here are that much more costly to put right in export markets.

Management information

Distribution, acknowledged as the only precise source of information on what has actually been sold, is the single best source of management information. International distribution with its wider span of control over the order cycle is a most important source of information in the firm. All too often this is not formally acknowledged and used. 'You can describe us as the central office of information in this firm' explained one shipping manager used to being the person senior management contacted when they could not discover the status of a particular order. Computer-based information systems, using data from a computerized order processing system, are now within the grasp of most firms. The shipping manager will need to ensure he gets good value from the firm's computing department.

Education and training

If one criticism only had to be levelled at exporting companies in general it would surely be about communication. In companies, with a dominant interest in their domestic market, export can seem both unimportant and all too complex. Mistakes are made by those who do not appreciate the peculiarities of export business. Sometimes export and shipping people themselves add to the mystique surrounding the subject and simultaneously add to the invisible barriers in the firm to smooth exporting.

The shipping manager is often home based rather than his ever absent sales colleagues but he is usually well experienced in the mechanics of exporting. A useful role for him is to take part in or initiate in-company training courses on the basics of exporting.

The shipping role has two components from a management perspective. The basic task of the role has to be completed, that of handling export orders efficiently within the firm and ensuring they are carried to the customer in the same way. The second component is the broader management task of influencing other business functions in developing a more systematic approach to international distribution.

Keypoints

1 A shipping manager has an unusually wide span of control especially if his department encompasses order processing as well as documentation and transportation.
2 Internally, the shipping department can be organized in a horizontal or vertical fashion.
3 A shipping manager needs to be able to influence others in the firm and can have a particular role to play in training.

5
Managing documentation

It is inappropriate in a text devoted to the management of international distribution to deal in depth with the detail of day-to-day activity. However the management of documentation is central to the international logistics function to the point where some detail is necessary for the practitioner to appreciate where the approaches being described relate to his day-to-day work and for the student to appreciate why it is necessary to spend considerable effort on what might appear at first sight a perfectly straightforward problem, the documentation of trade goods.

At the end of this chapter there is a brief summary of the nature of most of the major documents likely to be met by the trading company. A number of reference books are listed to provide access to a more rigorous coverage of individual documents and the documentation requirements of individual countries.

The documentation problem

Documentation for trade can be divided into four types:

Internal;
Financial;
Transportation;
Official.

As listed the four types increase in complexity when compared with the paperwork required for domestic trading. Internal documentation (works orders, customer records, etc.) will be prepared in almost the same way irrespective of whether the order is for a home or an export sale.

Financial documentation is more complex. A growing volume of trade is conducted on open account terms but the majority is still against some kind of documentary credit. This is likely to persist for two reasons. First, the basic lack of trust in trading with a foreign buyer. While you might trust the buyer himself, the exporter often requires the financial protection afforded by a documentary credit to protect against, for example, government action on trade. Second, dealing in documentary credits has significant cash flow advantages when trading with a distant market. Bills can be discounted against a bill of lading.

Transportation documentation has to be prepared more carefully to avoid delays and to ensure that transport documents, such as the bill of lading are correctly handled so that the right person has title to the goods at the right time.

Few domestic transactions require official documentation. All international transactions do. Errors in the completion of official documents may result in fines, delays or both.

The problem of documentation has five main components (Figure 16): complexity; culture; change; cost; and error.

Complexity	Numbers of documents and correspondents
Culture	Language, currency, law
Change	Changes in requirements
Cost	Costs of preparation
Error	Consequential costs of error and cost of correction

Figure 16   The problem of documentation.

Complexity

Even in a relatively routine international transaction, fifteen or so separate parties can be involved and the necessary information has to be supplied at just the right time for up to

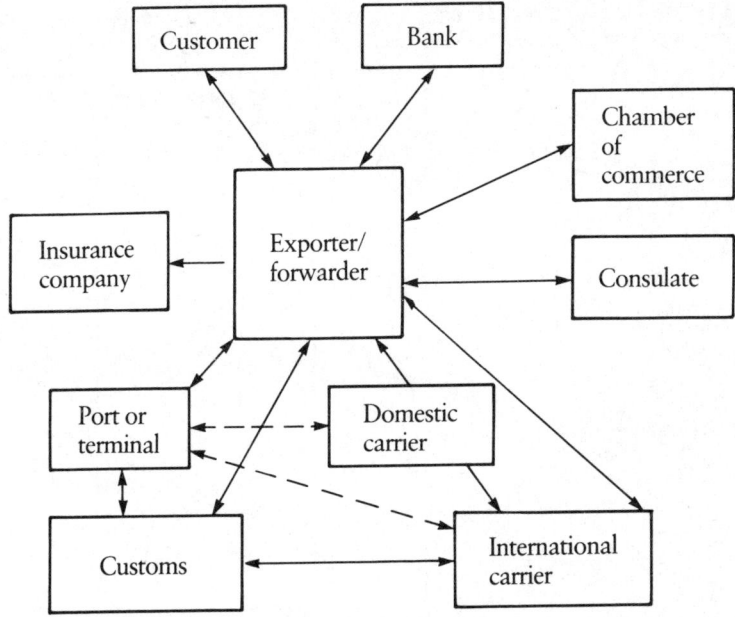

Figure 17 Main lines of communication in trade.

fifty commercial and official procedures. Figure 17 identifies the main lines of communication in international trade. The responsibility for documentation is divided between exporter and forwarder but for the purposes of discussion can be considered as a single role.

Table 1 identifies many of the documents that form part of these lines of communication and the body who normally prepares each.

Culture

National differences may make for enjoyable foreign vacations but they also add to the complexities of trade. The commercial invoice together with any packing list forms the basis of many trade documents. Simple enough perhaps but some countries demand as many as eight copies of the commercial invoice, others demand that the document be in their language or that any declarations be in their language.

Table 1

Range of International Trade Documents. From 'Computers and International Trade Documents' SITPRO 1981.

Document	Prepared by			
	Exporter	Forwarder	Carrier or Agent	Other
Order Processing				
Quotation	•			
Sales order	•			
Order acknowledgement	•			•
Packing list	•			
Despatch advice	•			
Credit note	•			•
Invoicing and Declarations				
Export invoice	•			
Customs invoice	•			
Certificate of Origin	•			
EUR Certificates	•			
Consular invoices	•			
Banking				
Documentary collection	•			
Letters of Credit				
Bills of Exchange	•			•
Insurance				
Insurance application	•			
Insurance certificates	•	•		•
Customs				
Export/declaration	•	•	•	
Import declaration	•	•	•	
Removal note		•	•	•
Shipping Instructions				
Standard shipping note	•	•		
Shipper's letter of instruction	•			
Export consignment note	•	•		
Application for space	•	•	•	
Shipping instructions (containers)	•	•		
Transport Documents				
Bill of Lading/Liner W/Bill	•	•	•	
Air Waybill/House Air W/B	•	•	•	
Road consignment note	•	•	•	
Rail consignment note	•	•	•	
Certificate of posting	•			
Postal documents	•			
Combined transport documents		•		
Dangerous goods documents	•			
EEC T forms	•	•		
Manifests			•	
Freight invoice		•	•	

Legal systems vary from one country to the next and over time. It can matter a great deal as to whose legal system pertains to a particular transaction. The interpretation of a phrase can vary between systems.

Only one-third of British exports are invoiced in a foreign currency. Rapidly changing exchange rates have been a feature of recent years and foreign exchange management is a subject on its own. Whether a company chooses to use another currency has a significant effect on any computerized documentation system (*see* Chapter 6).

Business practice varies between countries. Thirty days credit may be normal in one country while in another they may expect ninety days.[1]

Change

Changes in the number, type and content of documentation are all too frequent. Any attempt to systematize documentation must be flexible enough to accommodate change.

Cost

In 1973 and 1976 the British Simplification for International Trade Procedures Board (SITPRO) commissioned a study into the costs of handling export documentation. The results were summarized in the form of a formula linking the cost to the Retail Price Index. The cost per consignment for an exporter not using an aligned system (see later) is given by

$$\frac{£(28.23 \times \text{Current RPI})}{155.2}$$

By 1982 this put the cost per consignment at nearly £60. This cost, SITPRO claimed, based on the study results, could be halved by moving to an aligned system. Even so the costs of handling the complexity of export documentation are still high.[2]

Error

The statistics on error rates in documentation are frightening: there is no other word for it. What constitutes an error is often a matter of judgement and errors *can* be unimportant. But errors result in delays to goods, in contracts becoming technically void and in time-consuming alterations. The often quoted example of a Letter of Credit which contained a mis-spelling for the goods serves as a good illustration. The Bill of Lading, when issued, had to contain the same mis-spelling to present the Credit to the Bank.

The Documentation problem requires a number of factors for its solution: up-to-date knowledge; a method of eliminating or at least minimizing errors and; a method of minimizing cost. The easy answer is to rely upon the freight forwarder to provide a specialist service. But with the trend towards an in-house function many companies have to face the problem themselves.

Aligned documentation

During the 1950s the first aligned series of export documents were introduced in Scandinavia. Their success prompted the formation of a working party by the Economic Commission for Europe of the United Nations. They produced a design basis for almost all documents used in international trade, the ECE Layout Key. The first aligned systems were introduced into Britain in 1965 by the Board of Trade. Soon afterwards SITPRO were formed as one of a number of national bodies throughout the world concerned with simplifying trade procedures, the COMPROS.

The concept of alignment can be demonstrated graphically as in Figure 18. The two document series each consist of three documents. Each document in both series contains some information that is also on another document. In Series 1 the same data appears in precisely the same part of the page on each document. For example the exporters' name and address could be represented by box A, the importers' name and address by Box C and so on. The document series is 'aligned',

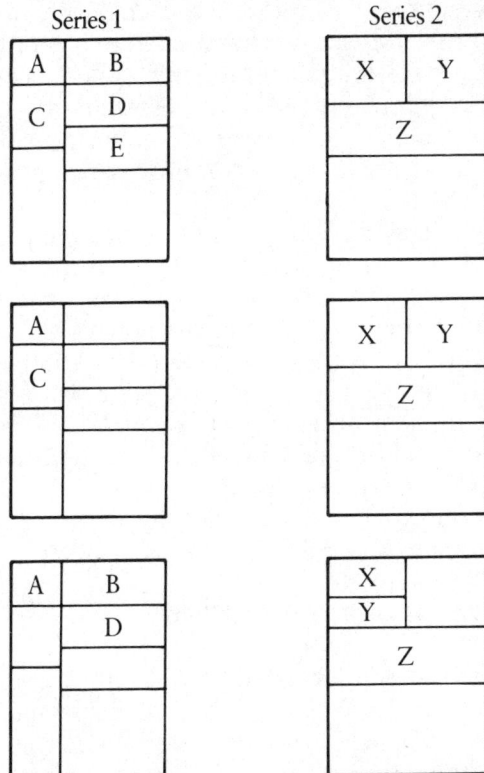

Figure 18 The aligned concept.

all the data in common appears in the same fashion in the same area of the page. The first document in the series could well be the master document for the series, that is the one original document on to which all the data for the document series is typed. The second and third documents can be produced from the master document by using overlays or screens to block out the information which is not needed while photocopying the master to produce the other documents. Both subsequent documents may well need fixed information (headings, standard declarations, etc.) which can either be preprinted on to the blank documents or printed on to the overlays, and the information has only been typed the once.

In the second series of documents each document contains, in fact, the same information but it is either in a different part of the document or it is given a different layout. There is little alternative to typing out each document separately. Each has to be checked and there are three times as much chance of error and nearly three times the cost of producing a single master document.

This example brings out the two disadvantages of alignment: the master document has to hold all the information, and secondly the system will only work when the documents to be prepared are designed to a common, aligned format. A carrier may however have his own documentation prepared to his own format (perhaps using the concept of alignment) which is not compatible to the exporter's. Both disadvantages have answers: a master document can be extended by using a flap to extend the master form; and gradually the COMPROS bodies are working towards the alignment of all export documentation to a common format.

The future for documentation

Ultimately the speed in which delivery is effected is controlled by the time taken to prepare documents and to undertake the formalities associated with them. As transit times reduce so documentation must keep pace. The computerization of trade data is perhaps inevitable.

Procedures associated with processing trade data, be it hard copy or electronic impulse, need to be refined and adapted to changes in the way freight is managed. For example, the approach of reverse integration outlined in Chapter 3 has the drawback that documentation has to be signed by the exporter, although the procedures are being handled almost entirely by his agent.[3]

With the advances in electronic technology and the rapid decline in the real price of data processing equipment, the need for hard copy documents may well decline in favour of computer-stored data and electronic data transmission. In the meantime the shipping manager has to be something of an expert on export documentation, what is needed for each country, each transport mode, each type of commodity. Fortunately reference books exist which are updated regularly,[4] leaving the manager with more time to consider the merits of alignment.

The next chapter looks at how the new technology will change the way an export office is run. These changes are already occurring in the larger firms. Other companies still retain perfectly efficient manual systems.

These manual systems normally rely upon two factors: documentation for the next order to an export customer is likely to be similar if not the same as for the last order; and a systematic checklist.

Companies evolve their own checklists for export consignments or purchase one of the commercial systems on offer. Filing cabinets are the hallmark of the shipping office with back-orders kept to hand to guide the shipping clerk in processing future orders.

This approach may sound Dickensian. However it must be remembered that export orders, of high repeat order goods, tend to be much larger than domestic orders. A given volume of turnover comes from fewer orders which are more complex to process and document.

The main export documents

The bill of lading

The Bill of Lading (BOL) has three functions:

(*a*) Evidence of receipt of specified goods;
(*b*) Evidence of contract of carriage;
(*c*) Certificate of title to the Goods.

In a transaction involving a documentary collection the exporter sends the BOL to the importer's bank, often via his own bank, for the former bank to release the BOL to the importer once payment has been cleared. The BOL then takes on its role as a document of title to allow the importer to collect his goods.

The BOL has acted as proof that the goods have been

received by the carrier i.e. they have left the control of the exporter. It also acts as part of the contract between the carrier and whoever is paying the freight. If the carrier is not satisfied as to the goods presented to him (short shipment, damage, etc.) he can 'clause' the BOL and in doing so possibly negate the value of the BOL as a document of title.

If the BOL does not reach the importer before the ship docks (because of delays in the banking system for example) the goods may attract demurrage at the docks. The BOL is also governed by international law.

The short form bill of lading (sea)

The short form BOL is a recent development which can appear under a number of different titles. It is a receipt of shipment only but is valuable because it does not delay the movement of goods. It is therefore attractive in trade with subsidiaries or long-standing customers where trust exists and there is no requirement for a documentary credit. It is not a certificate of title to the goods.

The commercial invoice (all modes)

The key export document is the commercial invoice. It is the basis of the transaction between buyer and seller and, apart from any shipping note or signature to another document, is the only documentation an exporter need prepare himself. The contents include all the data necessary to complete the majority of export documentation which can be undertaken by a forwarder. A single order with more than one item will require a packing list as part of, or as an extension to the invoice.

Certificate of origin/value (all modes)

Many countries are concerned about the country of origin of goods they receive, others are concerned for reasons of exchange control and customs that the correct value is declared. Exporters are often required therefore to provide certification of the origin of goods and their value. A number of documents fall into this category.

Consignment notes (all modes)

Delivery notes, Standard Shipping Notes (SSN) and 'bills of lading' (not ships' Bills of Lading) are all terms for various types of consignment notes. Frequently the terms are used synonymously although the Shipping Note is specifically for sea movements. They act as instructions to move goods.

The airway bill

The airway bill is the consignment note used for airfreight. It is often referred to as an air consignment more emphasizing that it is not a negotiable document as is the Sea Bill of Lading.

Certificates of Shipment

Certificates of Shipment are frequently issued by forwarders to confirm that goods have been received. Expressions such as house bill are also used. A received for shipment bill of lading issued by a shipping line is a similar document which does not have the standing of a full Bill of Lading.

T forms

Although the EEC is a free trade area it has spawned its own set of documentation. The T form series is used for goods moving within the EEC and has a similar role to the TIR carnet which facilitates the movement of goods by road trailers between countries. Their effect is that goods moving across intermediate borders, or within a country to be cleared by customs at an inland customs point, can travel freely without customs inspection until they reach their destination.

Customs documentation

Customs formalities vary from country to country and in the way they are applied. There is a greater need to record imports than exports because of any duty and quotas applicable. The data gathered by Customs is not always for their own use. Trade associations and Government departments are frequently keen to obtain information on market trends. The declaration of goods in the wrong tariff heading is a frequent error.

Keypoints

1 Documentation falls into one of four types: internal; financial; transportation; and official.
2 The problem of documentation has five main components: complexity; culture; change; cost; and error.
3 A systematic approach to documentation, namely alignment, can reduce cost, errors and simplify the documentation problem.

References and further reading

1 HEWSON, T. L. 'Notes on Western Europe' private publication for the Institute of Credit Management (current edition).
2 SITPRO 'Systematic Export Documentation' (SITPRO, London 1976).
3 SITPRO 'The Future for Export Documentation' (SITPRO, London 1980).
4 *See* for example, *Croners Reference Book for Exporters* (Croners, Surrey) (current edition).

6
Computerization

Most books about computing published after the middle to late 1970s use the word revolution either in their title or liberally in their text. The popular press and the business press have both been full, at one time or another, of articles predicting the end of society as we now know it. De-industrialization of society and the start of the age of leisure is one theme. De-industrialization and anarchy, because of mass unemployment, is another.

It is remarkable to recall that the microprocessor chip was developed as recently as 1971, by Intel Corporation in the USA. None of the dramatic increases in unemployment seen at the beginning of the next decade could be ascribed to the micro-revolution but forecasters were still insistent about its long-term effect on employment prospects.

The effect of the microchip was two-fold. The microchip made computing in its broadest sense orders of magnitude cheaper than in the days of traditional mainframe computers, full as they were of valves and literally miles of wiring, and sited in specially air-conditioned rooms. It also made computers much smaller and more robust, small and durable enough to put a powerful machine into the average office.

Because of the sometimes ill-informed and highly speculative comments in the media, the microchip seemed to threaten the livelihoods of very many people employed in manual and semi-skilled tasks. Yet the microchip was only one stage in the introduction of computers and any change in employment only one stage in what has occurred over the centuries.

On either side of the Atlantic there has been a similar pattern in the proportion of people in various employments. Well prior to the industrial revolution the majority were employed in agriculture. As society industrialized, employment patterns changed in favour of manufacturing industry. With the development of mass production techniques and, much more recently, computerized techniques, the proportion employed in manufacturing declined. Employment in distribution, wholesaling and retailing expanded as did other service industries. It is interesting to note that employment in a service occupation has always been fairly high, although historically 'service' often implied domestic service, being employed as the servant of an affluent class.

It is highly unlikely that the microchip will produce long-term structural unemployment but more likely that new employment areas will evolve. Already, within manufacturing companies, there has been a discernible trend towards a reduction in clerical and production jobs, but often in favour of other roles, those associated with the handling of information.

Nevertheless changes within any firm and changes in employment opportunities will not be achieved without some problems. Training and retraining constitute one vital area in answering the inevitable challenges. The attitude of organized labour is yet another factor.

Export and import distribution is largely a clerical function that has been associated with the employment of many, relatively low paid, white collar workers. The savings noted from adopting the concept of aligned documentation in Chapter 5 are substantially associated with savings in clerical labour costs.

It can be expected that further savings will result from a wider use of computer technology. However the use of a computer, in order processing and in documentation, means employing someone else with a higher level of skill to design, implement and support a computer system. Furthermore computerizing order processing greatly expands the opportunities to evolve a management information system. While the larger firms will have installed computerized order processing using the first generation of computer equipment, the reduction in cost of the new machines means that many more firms will now be computerizing their systems. Many firms will feel forced to computerize, not because of large labour savings, but because computerization would be necessary to match the service levels achieved by competitors who have moved from a manual system. The purpose of this chapter is to draw attention to the possibilities which already exist and those in computing which seem most likely to evolve of relevance to the international logistics function. Simultaneously the people problems of implementing any such innovations have to be considered.

The shipping office of the future

Computer technology is not only relevant to order processing and documentation but also to information flows and communication between people. Any shipping department will be a heavy user of mail, telephone and telex services. Gradually electronic mail services and facsimilie transmission will replace most mail services. Those firms who cannot afford their own high technology equipment will use specialist service firms who can. The freight forwarder may be as much concerned with offering advice and services in electronic data processing as he is today in documentation.

Figure 19 shows the typical export office with its links to some of the people with whom employees need to deal. Many of the tasks will change as will the methods of dealing with the outside links. Figure 20 shows one possibility for the office of the future.

Telephones could be replaced by videophones making face to face meetings less necessary. Letters will be typed into the shipping department's own computer terminal acting as a word processor. The letter will be addressed electronically by a device attached to the computer which will direct the communication to the recipient to be printed out on his computer printer. A letter which might have taken days to be delivered will be delivered in minutes. A meeting which might be extremely costly to arrange could take place within hours of

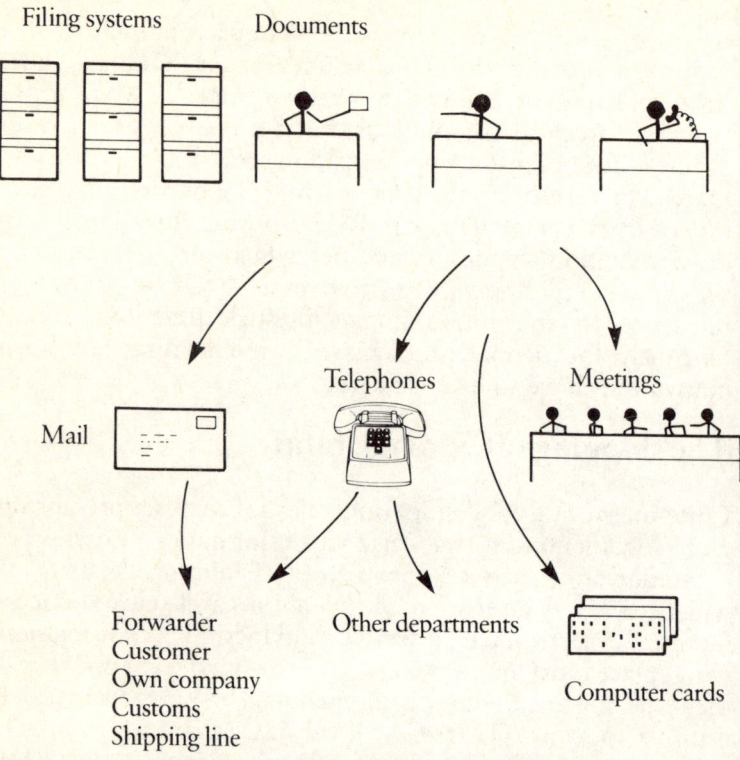

Figure 19   The traditional shipping office.

being called via videophone. A sales representative could make a detailed presentation of his company's freight services to a client without either having to leave his office.

The individuals in the shipping, export or import office need different skills when a computerized system is installed. The job satisfaction of some declines as the complexity of a manual, clerical system, supported perhaps by a batch process on a computer, is replaced by a real time system. There is no longer the necessity for keeping filing cabinets full of data on past shipments. A single computer data storage device weighing a few grammes can replace the contents of a number of filing cabinets.

A change in approach also means a larger role for some

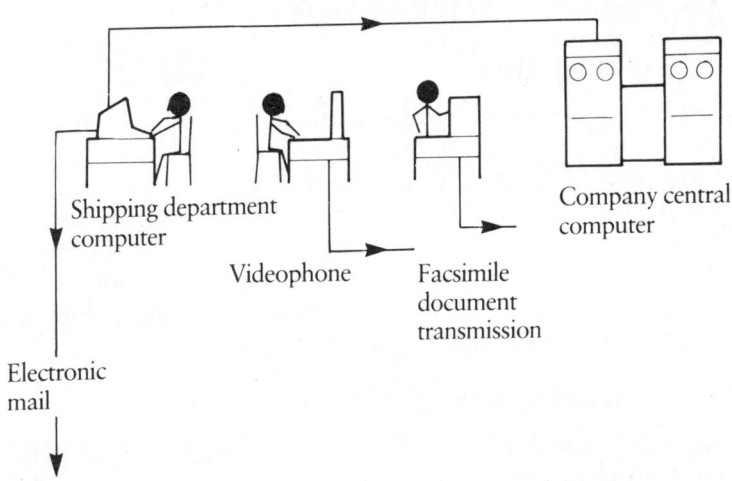

Figure 20   The computerized shipping office.

present employees. The shipping manager still needs to understand the computer system which has replaced his clerical system so that the new system can evolve with the same flexibility as before. He needs the same knowledge as he did previously but the change has meant he has the opportunity to spend more time appraising what is happening. At a touch of a button he can obtain an up-to-date picture of the number of outstanding orders, the freight bills to a particular market and much more.

It may soon be possible in many countries to book freight space by interrogating a national or even international data bank to see what capacity is available on a given vessel (or even lorry) and make a direct booking through the same data bank.

The smaller company who cannot afford the equipment and the computer programmes essential to this innovation will again rely on outside specialists who will have such a capability.

Computerized export systems

Why computerize?

Export logistics has three elements which can benefit from the use of a computer: order processing, documentation and information. Potentially a computer system can save money by replacing a clerical system with an electronic system, save time on order processing and therefore provide the customer with a better service, save both time and money by reducing the incidence of error, and allow for better decision-making and control by providing better information.

The scope of the system

A computer system is unlikely to be designed and installed by the shipping department's own personnel. To ease communication with the inevitable computer specialist a necessary first stage is to attempt to define fairly carefully what any system should do.

The simplest system of any value is a documentation system which will print individual shipping documents or one or more aligned master documents which can subsequently be used to produce document series via a photocopier or spirit duplicator. A suitable computer would include those machines dedicated to the manipulation of text (rather than data processing or calculation) called word processors. A more sophisticated, and more expensive, system will handle order processing with the ultimate being a system capable of handling stock control, production planning and order processing and documentation for both home and overseas sales.

The choice between systems will depend primarily upon the products being handled and the volume of orders. The more the company deals with repeat order products and the more consignments it handles the more attractive will be the ultimate system.

Another consideration is whether the new system can run on a computer the firm already uses and whether it can be made compatible with any existing systems that it might have to share data with, for example, data on the availability of stock, with a domestic order processing system.

Software and hardware

Software, the computer programmes that instruct the computer and its various peripheral parts (together with the 'computer hardware') can be obtained in a number of ways.

The easiest method is to purchase an existing set of programmes (a package) written with enough content and flexibility to cope with the objectives established by the shipping department when defining the scope of their required system.

By 1982 very few packages had ever been written for export shipping. There were a number available for export documentation and a large number available for domestic order processing.

Domestic order processing is more suitable for computerization. Typically, for the manufacturer of high repeat order products, the problem is how to cope with a large number of relatively similar tasks. On export the number of order entries is comparatively small for the same value of business as the manufacturer is selling mainly to agents or distributors rather than directly to retailers or users. The problem on export is more to assemble a great deal of information with a high degree of flexibility. Demands for the system to cope with different currencies and languages add significantly to the complexity.

Many attempts in the 1970s to write a software package which would be suitable for a large number of companies failed. Such is the status of distribution in many firms that it is difficult to get priority over other functions for the time of computer specialists to write a special programme.

By 1982 only a quarter of British companies offering international forwarding services had a computer system capable of handling documentation.

Despite estimates that nearly half of all shipping offices in the UK could justify, on a cost reduction basis alone, the installation of a computer system, only a small minority of traders were using them for international orders. The one

British company offering a computer bureau service to exporters (clients' data was run on their computers) became insolvent at the end of 1981 because of lack of demand for their services.

The computer revolution was very slow in coming to export distribution.

Computerizing export logistics

It is likely that an existing package marketed by a specialist software company will need considerable 'tailoring' to suit the exporter in this complex area. In this instance, and where no package is available to suit the shipper's needs, the software will be an expensive item. While the cost of hardware has tumbled the cost of software, a labour-intensive product, has not.

Many software companies market a range of hardware and many hardware companies produce software or have a link with a software company. Problems of compatibility can arise when running programmes on one machine which were designed to run on another. This results in additional expense as the software has to be tailored for the new equipment.

The type of contract a software house will offer on a business system ranges from just the supply of a computer package to the definition of a computer system, writing the software, supplying and installing the computer, training staff and maintaining the system (fault finding, reprogramming to update the system for minor changes).

The narrower the scope of the system the less likely is the need for the latter type of service. As computers and computer programming become more a part of everyday life, even in the home, the use of well written programmes by the informed non-specialist without outside help becomes ever more feasible.

With the reducing cost of hardware has come the ability to change from the traditional method of running computer programmes, batch processing, to real time operation. In batch processing, data is fed into a computer only at a set time, often by a specialist department. In real time processing the programme is normally constantly available to the user via his own computer terminal or visual display unit (VDU), a combined keyboard and screen. By the mid 1970s real time was considered to be the standard approach. However many companies would still be using a batch system, devised before this time or, because they are a small firm, a batch system via a computer bureau.

The export system

Figure 21 identifies the export system of a manufacturer of high repeat order products. The model incorporates the main points of a number of systems evolved by British companies. Any computer system designed to support the export system fully would begin after the initial stock pool has been defined, although it is possible to computerize sales forecasting to provide a production schedule in some firms.

To understand the practical implications of Figure 22 it is useful to consider the very simple example of a firm producing and marketing only two products, A and B, and selling them in markets 1, 2, 3 and 4. Market 1 is the firm's domestic market. A different language and a different legal system are used in each of the four markets. The firm's production line can manufacture either A or B but not both simultaneously. The longer the production run the lower the firm's costs because of the time taken to switch from one product to another.

The export salespeople together with the firm's agents in markets 2, 3 and 4 have estimated what they can sell in the next month. So have the home salespeople. The total sales forecast was 100 tonnes of A and 200 tonnes of B. However 10 tonnes of B is for markets 3 and 4 who need different outer packaging on both product and cases. (The company has managed to standardize packaging in other markets and in all markets for product A.)

The most cost-effective way of dealing with the packaging problems of product B is to relabel standard product rather than to switch production to different packaging. By doing this the company has no need to hold separate stocks of special

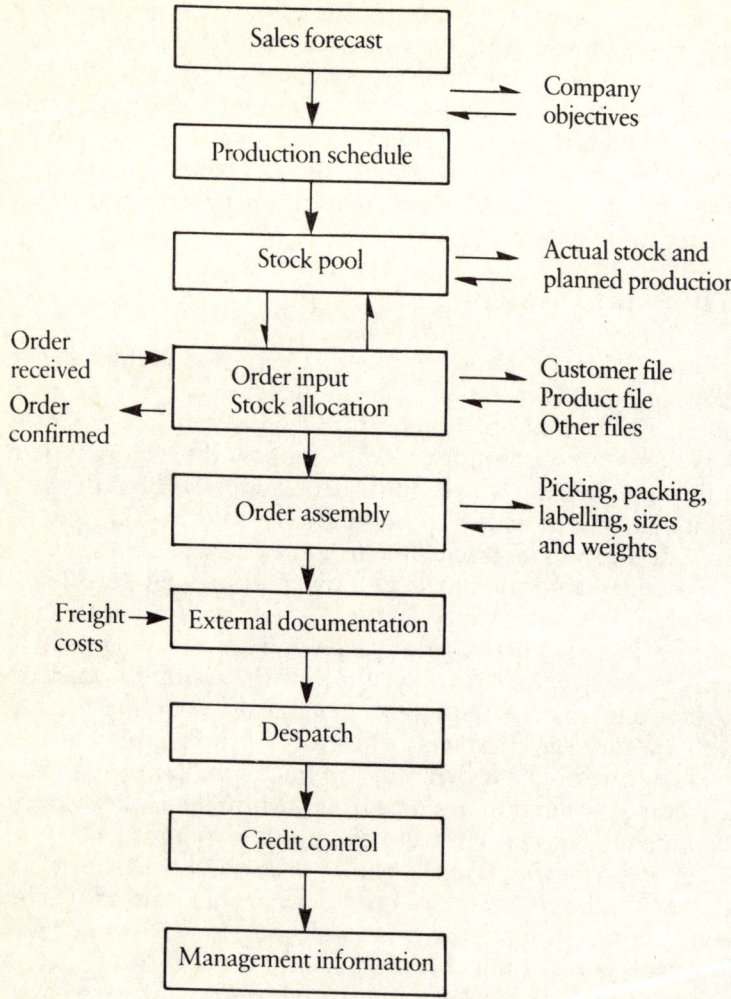

Figure 21   Stages in a computerized export system.

products. Currently stocks of A stand at 50 tonnes and stocks of B at 200 tonnes. This excludes stock already allocated to domestic or export orders.

The long-term forecast of demand for A and B indicates an increase in demand for A. Consequently, the production planning team set a target of increased stock of A and decreased stock of B. They can produce at the rate of up to 350 tonnes each month and schedule production of 200 tonnes of A and 100 tonnes of B, expecting month end stocks of 150 tonnes of A and 100 tonnes of B (Table 2).

Table 2
Simplified Production Schedule

Product	A (tonnes)	B (tonnes)
Current stocks (a)	50	200
Planned stocks (b) at month end	150	150
Sales forecast (c)	100	200
Planned production (d) (c) + (b) − (a)	200	150
Stock Pool (a) + (d)	250	350
True stock pool	250	Regular 340 Special pack 10

The current stock and the planned stock together constitute what is called the stock pool which can be allocated to orders during the coming month by either home or export sales, with one complication: that stocks of B for markets 3 and 4 have to be repacked (10 tonnes). Assuming this is also scheduled then the maximum of B that can be offered for sale during the next month is 340 tonnes plus 10 tonnes of special pack, and of A a maximum of 250 tonnes (Table 2).

During the month orders are received for home and export sales. A check is first made as to whether the company can meet the order from its stock pool and then whether stocks actually in existance are adequate for the order. If the answer is positive for both then the order is accepted and stock allocated to the order by the system.

If orders arrive more quickly than expected then the order may have to be placed against mainly or even totally planned production (which does not exist as yet as finished goods) and the customer advised of any delay.

Two obvious problems can occur. What happens when the actual sales to one market exceed forecast and what happens when total sales exceed the stock pool?

The policies which firms adopt vary. Some limit the orders accepted to the total predicted by each market and some to the total of all sales predicted. Thus if a large domestic order of 250 tonnes of B arrived, some systems would allow the order because stock is available. Some would not because it exceeds the domestic sales forecast and denies stock to other markets. Any reallocation of stock would then be made by discussion between the different salespeople involved, the point being that the computer system cannot take the decision automatically to reallocate the stock pool between markets.

It is possible that more stock of B can be made available by rescheduling production or prolonging production of B using overtime. However it is often preferable to stick to a production schedule and avoid the cost of switching production lines between products.

Where the firm decides it cannot meet the order from the stock pool the customer cannot be given a firm delivery promise. Bearing in mind what was said earlier about delivery promises it is vital that the customer is given a satisfactory answer to his order. Most firms using the kind of system outlined here will issue an order confirmation, possibly with an estimated despatch or delivery date if an order can be allocated against the stock pool and a separate order acknowledgement to orders for which there is no actual stock or planned production.

One of the implications of Table 2 is that it is very much easier to manage order processing if the stock pool is enlarged by high permanent stocks. However because it costs money to hold stocks a balance has to be struck between stock levels and the possibility of losing custom because of an inability to meet orders. Ultimately it is the accuracy of the sales forecast which determines the ease of order processing for best stock level.

Part orders can be a problem with both domestic and export sales but more so with the latter. The existence of high minimum charges for freight penalizes the shipment of part orders but the customer might be happy with the situation if the supplier is selling from a delivered price list.

Perhaps the main problem faced by some firms in this area is the production scheduling decision when an order has been received subject to a letter of credit. The customer promises a letter of credit and the firm may have to produce a large volume of goods quickly to meet the terms. But what happens if the credit never arrives? The firm is left with what might be highly specialized product unsuitable for another market. Eventually the firm has to take a view on the likelihood of the order falling through or insist on the letter of credit prior to production scheduling.

Order entry

In using a real time system each domestic and export section has a VDU connected to the main computer system. The export order is checked to ensure the customer's credit status and the necessity or otherwise of a letter of credit. The order is then typed into the system and a check made on the stock available to ensure the order can be met. Alternatively the system itself will automatically refuse to accept part of or all of the order.

Some firms use the order number as a cross-reference to help assemble the data required during the order process. The order number may have a unique code followed by a code denoting the customer, another denoting the mode of transport, another the invoicing currency and so on.

The computer stores information against the order number so that at any stage the status of the order can be checked and any information stored against that number can be used to produce management reports.

If stock is available the complete order is typed into the file and an instruction sent to the warehouse to pick and pack the order. It is possible with some products to estimate automatically the final pack size and weights. These figures can be used to prebook space with a carrier awaiting confirmation of the precise data after packing.

Ideally the warehouse will have its own terminal and printer. The order for packing can be sent in seconds to the warehouse who can enter the final sizes and weights directly into the system, removing two opportunities for problems in communication between two departments. The full packing list can also be entered from the warehouse.

Most export consignments will need careful marking, often in more than one language. One of the few advantages of export order processing comes from dealing with a stable list of customers i.e. subsidiaries or agents whose requirements *vis-à-vis* case marking, packing and consignment can remain unchanged over long periods.

Assembling the necessary data

The advantage of a stable customer list can also be used to good effect in preparing the necessary documentation for despatch.

Terms of sale and trade are discussed in Chapter 9. One of the features of international trade is the variety of terms which can be used compared with the cash with order or open account terms which prevail in domestic trade. It is advantageous to agree *one* set of terms with a customer. These are entered into a computer file against his name. When an order number includes this particular customer's reference number, the data on terms of sale, address for consignment, special declarations necessary on documentation can be added to the order file automatically in a similar way to what happens in a manual system where it is customary to look up the last order sent to the consignee and duplicate the procedures followed previously. In the computer system such data is held on computer file.

Very few companies hold a price list for delivered pricing on exports. Most hold ex-works (i.e. domestic) or so called FOB prices (in practice domestic plus costs to the point of international carriage) on file. If the customer is being invoiced for a delivered price the freight cost has to be added to the commercial invoice, and this is normally done manually or by typing it in separately into the computer system. There are some advantages in entering freight costs into the computer system and retaining them, as they may provide a useful record, useful in predicting freight costs for budgeting purposes and for monitoring current expenditure against budget.

Estimating the freight cost is one way of providing a delivered price. The computer can be used to undertake this calculation. While this may be feasible for very regular traffic flows, and adequate for intra-company trading, it is unlikely to be a practical idea for most firms. A minority of companies selling very high value goods can hold delivered prices by market area because freight accounts for a small proportion of their selling price. Even they have the problem of estimating FOB values required for Customs declarations.

Insurance becomes more complex in international trade. Some countries refuse to accept CIF (cost, insurance and freight) contracts unless the insurance is effected in their own country. Many exporters decide to insure their exports themselves on C and F contracts. Most have blanket insurance policies in which they can advise their insurers retrospectively about consignments to be covered by the policy on a regular schedule. Insurance costs may be shown separately on an invoice and, like freight costs, have to be entered into the system or added manually at a later stage to the documentation.

Many documents have to carry declarations of one sort or another, often in the language of that country. Declarations can be computerized and called up using a code, the clerk has only to enter the code rather than type in an unfamiliar language.

It is difficult to generalize further about what every company will need to prepare its export documentation. Real time systems will tend to be written interactively, that is to say, designed to ask the user a series of questions about the export order to ensure that each stage specific to that company's business has been covered.

Producing documents

Companies with computerized systems rarely choose to print any individual export document directly from the computer system. Instead they tend to produce a master document which is screened to print subsequent documents via a photocopier or spirit duplicator. The master document should follow the principles of alignment discussed in Chapter 5. There is no reason why more than one master document should not be produced to make the task of copying over individual documents simpler as the extra cost for a computer to reprint data is small.

Printing individual documents *on* the computer requires either a printer dedicated to each document type or constantly changing the paper feed to process different documents. Much depends on how many consignments and documents are being produced as to which solution to adopt, but neither approach is advised.

The advantage of computer printing the aligned master document and producing other documents on a copier is very noticeable when multiple copies are required. Photocopiers with preprinted overlays built into a special attachment or feeding the machine with preprinted documents constitute the most widely adopted methods of document production.

Eventually computer printers will become widely available that can print not only the words and figures on to a preprinted document but also the document itself, the small print, rulings and titles. It is then feasible for the computer to be used to print many, if not all, documents directly on to blank paper. Only at this stage may it be advantageous not to produce master documents and photocopies.

Documentation systems

The discussion so far has centred on the more sophisticated order processing systems which are more suitable for high repeat order products. Many firms producing other product types or acting as import/export agents may decide to invest in a separate documentation system, a word processor and software package.

These 'stand alone' systems do not need to be connected to any order processing system, but can be. They can then be used to convert a system designed to process only domestic orders into one which can handle international documentation.

The documentation systems are often supplied as complete systems, software and hardware. Customer and product files are held on storage discs, other data is typed into the system for each order. These systems can be used to print aligned master documents or individual documents.

Such systems are more suitable for the smaller firm or the custom product firm where the volume of consignments is small. Another advantage of purchasing a stand alone device is that its use will not be limited to export or import administration. Justifying the purchase solely for documentation and for the administrative side of order processing (no links to stock control, warehousing, production scheduling) could be difficult but, if the word processing abilities of the equipment can also be used elsewhere in the firm, the purchase can be very cost effective.

Paperless information exchange

There are few reasons why many documents ever need to appear as hard copy and cannot remain as computer records. This extends to the interchange of information. In theory there is no reason why traders should not send data to forwarders, carriers or, in those countries that allow it, to customs, using computer storage devices (discs or tape) rather than paper records. However this is of limited value. Ideally the company would like to link its own computer to that of the other party to exchange data directly. The problem with either concept is the compatibility of the way data is used by both systems (computers like people speak in different languages and dialects). Standards have been designed for the transmission of trade data between computers and some countries already have customs computers which can be accessed directly (although rarely by traders). It is worth checking that any brought-in system does comply with the accepted national standards for data exchange.

The large multinational organizations have often installed direct links between subsidiaries in different countries for the interchange of data. Trade documentation is one element in this interchange. The firm may need to decide between facsimile transmission or data transmission. Facsimile is the process where a copy of the document is converted and coded into electronic signals to be decoded by the receiver into a copy of the document. However it is much simpler and therefore cheaper to send just the data on the form.

Management information

A benefit that is difficult to cost, which should be produced by computerization, is improved management information. A computer does not object to the routine task of collecting and collating a mass of statistics on orders received, in progress, despatched by market and mode of transport. Scanning such data gives a manager the opportunity to identify potential problems before they occur. It would be a mistake not to take advantage of the time saved by computerization and allow the shipping manager to spend time analysing the system for which he is responsible. Many managers have too little time to consider long-term developments as they are forever fire-fighting short-term problems. A computer system could be the opportunity for a change for the better in this one respect alone.

Keypoints

1 Computerizing an export system has the following benefits:

   (*a*) lower costs;
   (*b*) greater accuracy;
   (*c*) reduced need for file storage;
   (*d*) fewer errors;
   (*e*) faster order processing;

(*f*) better information for management;

(*g*) the installation of a systematic approach.

2 Computerization can cause the following problems:

(*a*) negative reaction from organized labour;

(*b*) redundancy of clerical staff;

(*c*) the changeover from manual to computer systems;

(*d*) the need for retraining;

(*e*) lack of compatibility between systems (standardization);

(*f*) the inflexibility of a system.

3 The choice of system ranges from a stand alone documentation system to a fully integrated order processing system.

4 The advent of computerization will change many of the day-to-day activities involving clerical tasks and communications.

References and further reading

VOSS, C. A. and SUBLER, R. J. 'The use of computers for Processing Shipping Documentation' (2nd edn) (Harbridge House, London 1978).

SITPRO 'Computers in International Trade and Transport – Data standards', Vols 1 and 2, (SITPRO, London 1978).

SITPRO 'Computers and International Trade Documents', (SITPRO, London 1981).

DAVIES, G. J. 'Computer Based Export Systems' in *International Logistics* (MCB, Bradford, 1981).

7
Purchasing freight services

An essential part of a shipping manager's role is the purchase of freight and forwarding services. Even the company who relies heavily on the traditional forwarder has the task of selection and monitoring. The shipping manager has to face two problems in this purchasing role: he is only a part-time buyer and the products he buys are difficult to specify.

Most professional buyers will draw up a specification for any product they wish to purchase. An industrial component will be required to achieve a certain standard of quality of performance, which can be quantified with some precision by a technologist or production manager. A specification for a service is more difficult to devise, especially as the recipient, the consignee, is rarely part of the buyer's own organization.

This chapter presents information on what is actually bought in freight and how it is bought with the objective of enabling the freight buyer to be more analytical in his purchasing.

In a survey of British shipping managers[1] in 1978 (which will be referred to throughout the chapter as the SSE survey) over 10% spent more than £1,000,000 each year on freight, however only 32.1% of those surveyed had a freight budget. Clearly there is a need for more concern about the purchasing of freight services than this latter figure implies.

How is freight purchased?

Most industrial purchases are not the sole responsibility of one individual. Some aspects of the purchase may be delegated, some may need to be referred up the management hierarchy. Many purchases made for one department may affect the work of another so their opinions may influence the purchase.

The term 'decision-making unit' (DMU) has been coined to be used instead of 'buyer' to represent the reality of the industrial purchase where more than one person can influence decision making. A useful method of categorizing a buying task is to identify who in the firm has one of two roles: The major decision-making role; and the role of being consulted about the decision. One survey for example found that 31% of the decisions on the mode of transport were made at director level.[2] The shipping manager is more likely to be in middle management (52.2% of the SSE survey described themselves as middle management) and any change in mode is likely to need sanction from a superior, for example a switch from surface to air.

Conversely the selection of carrier or forwarder from an approved list is often delegated. 51% of the SSE survey delegated some responsibility for selection to subordinates. Of those who did (or were able to) delegate, only 10.7% delegated total responsibility, 67.5% delegated the responsibility to choose from an approved list of companies, 74.6% looked to subordinates to nominate companies for approval and 56.3% delegated the task of monitoring the performance of forwarder or carrier.

The shipper is often very loyal to his forwarder or carrier, 32.4% of the SSE survey had been using their main forwarder or operator for ten or more years.

The freight market is relatively complex, a shipper can deal solely or partially through a forwarder, deal directly with a carrier, choose between modes and choose between a number of competing services in each mode.

One way of representing the way firms handle the complexity of the market is shown in Figure 22. In the first stage all possible choices are considered, at least in theory. In practice the buyer is rarely aware of all the possible choices. Those that he, or the DMU, are aware of, survive to the second stage. Here various choices are eliminated, sometimes in a relatively subjective way. Railfreight might be ignored because

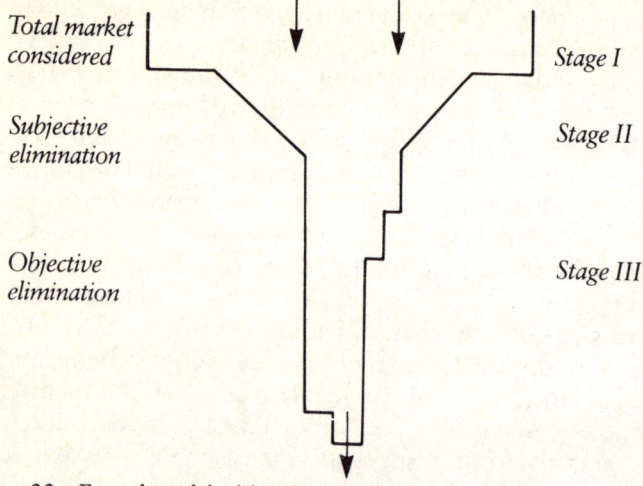

Figure 22   Funnel model of freight purchasing.

of 'a bad experience' many years previously. A manager may prefer to deal only through larger forwarding companies. Thus only a small proportion of the possible purchases enter the final stage when a number of relatively objective criteria will be used. Even so the process of selection is often a process of rejecting possibilities for one reason or another rather than weighing the benefits of all services at one time. Without a purchasing specification it is difficult to do otherwise.

The funnel model, based on the observation of the purchasing of a great many freight buyers, seems to imply a rather hit and miss process. In reality the buyer will usually select a perfectly adequate service. It might not be the best choice but when the buyer is spoilt for choice, finds it difficult to obtain reliable data on a service, and has other matters to attend to apart from freight buying, searching for the optimum choice is unlikely to be a priority.

The problem has two sides to it. The freight company with an excellent service has to ensure that his service is not excluded in Stages I or II and is well presented for consideration in Stage III. Secondly the exporter or importer may be spending too much on freight, or buying an inadequate or even an inappropriate service.

The industrial buyer often looks to avoid risks. Any change to a new forwarder or carrier has an associated risk. If the present supplier is adequate then why change? The buyer will frequently take sufficient risk to fulfil his role as a servant of his firm but will be wary of taking a larger risk which may damage his career. Many writers talk about the buyer as a risk avoider as opposed to a profit maximizer. The buyer has to be aware of the tendency to avoid making an error rather than looking always for the most cost-effective purchase and ensure that the accusation of being a risk-avoider does not apply to him.

Refining the buying process (Figure 23)

For regular traffic the buying process should consist of a series of well-defined stages. The first task is to define, with sales or with the customer, the level of service required. Different service levels mean different cost structures. A total distribu-

1 Define service level required
2 List possible services
3 Investigate transit times, costs, etc.
4 Produce short list
5 Invite sales presentations
6 Investigate facilities of final choice(s)
7 Use service on trial basis
8 Appraise against criteria defined in 1
9 Review performance with supplier

Figure 23   The buying process.

tion cost analysis will define the order of magnitude of service and cost but decisions between a premium groupage service or a regular groupage service, for example, are often too fine to be calculated. The maxim of the customer always being right is probably the most valid criterion to use to decide on the precise level of service to be purchased. If the customer wants it quickly then the premium service is more attractive.

The next stage is to list all or at least a broad cross-section of the possible choices. If a decision has not been made on service and price level then two or more separate lists need compiling. Each potential supplier is then invited to present their service. A short list can then be prepared and the service depot visited. The most promising service is then placed on trial, or if the business is large enough, two competing services are employed.

Transit times and the reliability of transit times have been identified as the main service criteria. The service(s) should be monitored against such criteria. It is only fair to inform the forwarder or carrier of the results and to make sure he realizes under what circumstances he can expect to lose the account.

The need to monitor freight bills against freight quotations may seem obvious but some firms find significant discrepancies between what they expect to pay for freight and what is invoiced. Surcharges in line with inflation might be acceptable but the sudden appearance of extra charges needs challenging. Monitoring the ratio of freight costs to weight over time is essential.

The author was retained by a company to evaluate the management techniques used by a large and successful exporter. In his opinion the shipping manager ranked relatively highly as a professional. Despite this, a casual evaluation of three consecutive invoices from one forwarder/operator showed a significant difference in the freight rates charged, the second in the series being much higher than the other two, and even these were barely compatible.

Because of the difference in number of packages in each consignment and marginal differences in the route each had moved over, a precise comparison was not possible. Nevertheless the company successfully challenged the forwarder/operator on the amounts charged.

Inconsistent charges

In one exporting company the shipping clerk was not required to check the freight invoiced against the freight quotations received prior to despatch. An accounts clerk in a different office was responsible for paying freight accounts. One weekend the shipping clerk came in on his own and happened to compare one freight invoice against the freight quotation he had received. The difference was significant. Nevertheless no new system was introduced to reconcile quotations against invoices or to monitor the invoice values over time. After all his status in the firm was such that he may not have felt able to point out a problem which affected another, more senior department.

Comparing quotations with invoices

The emergency order

Every firm has experienced the emergency order, the spare part needed to keep a machine going, the product sample necessary to clinch a major order. In many firms airfreight is used automatically to freight the emergency order. Because airfreight is relatively expensive, airfreighting regular orders often needs the approval of a senior executive. In contrast there is often a standing instruction to allow airfreight of emergency orders (possibly up to a certain weight) without individual approval.

A Civil Aviation Authority survey of shippers[3] indicated that the decision to airfreight was taken 30% of the time by consignees, 30% by consignors and as a joint decision otherwise. In the same survey shippers were asked to rank ten factors in order of importance relevant to the choice of airfreight. The 'need for urgent delivery' ranked first followed by 'specified by customer'. Interestingly 'other savings in total distribution costs' came last just behind 'cheaper than alternative transport'. Of those who did not use airfreight, 72% nominated the reason that air was 'too expensive' (rather than that they had no requirement for early delivery).

Many firms have undertaken total distribution cost analyses that demonstrate the benefits of using air rather than surface to serve a market, usually a distant market. However the use of airfreight to serve near markets, for example in inter-European trade, has been questioned by those who believe that (certain) surface transport is better placed to achieve reliably fast delivery compared with the normal airfreight system.

Some 90 to 95% of airfreight is handled by the airfreight forwarders. In most countries the airforwarder, to claim agency from the airlines, has to be registered by IATA (the International Air Transport Association). However an agent can sell airfreight services without an IATA licence by acting as a sub-agent for a licensed firm.

The majority of airfreight consignments travel in an agent's consolidation. Consolidations from an individual agent rarely leave every day on any one route, although some agents pool their consignments to increase the frequency of departure. 80% of airfreight travels in passenger aircraft bellyhold.

It is not unusual for an 'emergency' consignment to be accepted by a sub-agent, delivered to an IATA agent at a regional airport, trucked to a major airport, consolidated, airfreighted, deconsolidated, cleared by the consolidator, handed to the consignee's clearance agent for delivery to the consignee. Although this is an extreme example it does illustrate the potential for error and delay in the complexity of the airfreight system.

Premium (rather than consolidated) airfreighting is, on the other hand, potentially very fast e.g. if the consignor presents the consignment at the airport, pays for a next flight out service and advises the consignee of the flight number for him to pick the consignment up at the airport. Nevertheless the normal airfreight consignment travels via a consolidation.

The door-to-door transit times achieved by the normal airfreight system on shorthaul destinations often compare unfavourably with transit times achieved by a door-to-door road service, which is also potentially a much cheaper service. The question remains: why do traders use airfreight for time-sensitive consignments to short-haul markets?

Part of the answer could be in the way firms process emergency orders. For an ex-stock item the time taken between receiving an order and its being ready for despatch can be a few working days. In contrast an emergency order can be handled in hours.

Frequently the consignee specifies airfreight (after all it is his emergency), or else the standing order to airfreight emergency consignments means airfreight is used automatically by the consignor. Despite the problems inherent in the airfreight system the consignment reaches the consignee faster than a normal consignment reaching him by road but largely because of improved order processing.

A survey by Gray[4] in 1979 asked British shipping managers about their perception of door-to-door transit times from the UK to Europe using different transport modes. The mean time for less than full load traffic by road vehicle was found to be 6.7 days and for air 3.2 days.

A small survey by the author of European sales people (attending an exhibition in Geneva in 1981) indicated that salespeople expected a similar door-to-door service of 7 days by road but a faster air service of 1–2 days.

In 1982 a detailed study by the author designed to compare the actual times achieved by airfreight consolidation and one of the daily scheduled road freight services, revealed average door-to-door times for the former which could not be distinguished from airfreight consolidation at a much reduced cost.

Incidentally it proved very difficult to obtain a precise measure of departure and arrival times for consignments emphasizing the problems that a freight buyer would have without any additional resources to appraise the performance of any freight service.

Since the 1970s there has been a growth in daily, scheduled road services in Europe, some offering guaranteed money back transit times of 24 hours within the European heartland and 48–72 hours elsewhere. Other services, using own account rather than scheduled airlines, have also been launched.

Perceptions of transit times

As 'Perceptions of transit times' indicates, the purchase of an express freight service is complicated by the perceptions of both shippers and salespeople, the differences between what is perceived and achieved and differences in perception between the two roles. There is little doubt that the basis for the decision to airfreight emergency orders in Europe, and by inference in other short-haul markets, can be questioned. This example emphasizes the need for a quantitative appraisal of any freight service.

So what does the freight purchaser buy?

No one list of factors can be drawn up to describe each and every purchasing decision made by a freight buyer or the decision-making unit of which he forms a part. In Britain the role of shipping manager is fairly well-defined while in other countries there is no parallel role, freight buying being dealt with as part of a sales administration function for example.

Trying to generalize about freight buying may not seem to be a particularly fruitful activity. But, without analysing the buying process, it is difficult to improve upon buying habits. Because something is complex does not mean that no useful generalizations can be made.

There are two views of the industrial buyer. The first has him as a totally rational individual who has all the necessary information to enable him to make a totally informed decision. This view of the 'economic' buyer implies that, over time, only the most appropriate and cost effective services will be purchased in any quantity. The example of the way the emergency order is handled in practice is but one piece of evidence to show that the idea of the freight buyer as a truly 'economic' buyer does not describe reality.

An alternative picture of the freight buyer is that each buyer acts with a mixture of rationale and emotional motives. Clearly he is not consciously emotional about any purchase and each purchase can be rationalized.

One academic researcher into freight purchasing and one of the few to study international rather than domestic freight buying[5] used the expression 'subjective rationality' to describe the freight purchase. In his view each buyer builds a picture of the freight market, based on knowledge, experience and personal perception in his mind which he uses to make his buying decisions. Frequently the data used to build this picture is perceived rather than actual. While the buyer truly believes he is making a logical decision, he is deciding using a faulty model of the market from which he is buying.

The author conducted a study of exporters in the Manchester area on behalf of a forwarder/operator who offered groupage services to and from a number of European countries and Britain. Part of the work involved asking shipping managers about the freight services they were already using. Frequently the exporting companies were sending consignments to similar destinations in continental Europe from the Manchester area. Where they made the decision on the forwarder/operator who carried their goods, most buyers used the expression 'they are *the* specialists' to describe the service of their choice and as one of the reasons for using that particular service.

Surprisingly no two buyers (in the small survey of 25 companies) used the same service to the same destinations. Either Manchester is blessed with many specialist freight companies or, as is more likely, each buyer was satisfied with the service he received but sought to justify his decision by the use of the term 'specialist' to indicate that no better choice was available to him.

Justifying a buying decision

Some researchers have concentrated on trying to evolve lists of factors which are important in making buying decisions in domestic and international freight. What has been said already about a buyers' 'subjective rationality' leads one to doubt whether any such list can predict with any precision what will be the reaction of a freight buyer to a given freight service in any given circumstance. Nevertheless all the research has two factors in common: the price charged is rarely, if ever, the sole determining factor and one or more service elements are usually the most critical factors.

Figure 24 contains the results of one such study on American traffic managers. The seven factors are listed in order of their importance. Each 'factor' consists of more than one element. For example speed and reliability are linked apparently and in practice are considered together. What the customer feels appears in more than one factor. Given the difficulty of measuring arrival times the main measure of satisfactory transit times is whether or not the customer complains. Frequently the 'customer' is another distribution manager who also has his subjective picture of the freight market. His opinion, as well as his actual experience of the freight service, is obviously relevant.

The list of factors after price contains a number of items which are not included in lists offered by other writers and excludes a number which are (attitudes to small consignments, whether the company is local, how large they are, the quality of the salesperson, what type of equipment they offer). Each buyer will have his own factors, which may not be important to other buyers but because of his particular product, or even his own particular preconceptions, are important to him. No one list can contain each and every factor. There will always be factors which are important to a minority or are of minor importance to a majority. But the major factors are invariably speed and reliability.

Speed and reliability (transit times, pick up delivery reliability, reliable transit times, customer satisfaction)

Freight rates (competitive rates, low rates, controlled costs)

Loss and damage

Company policy and customer influence

Inventory levels (especially in mode choice)

Market competitiveness

External market influences

Figure 24   Factors in freight choice. *Source*: McGinnis, M. A. *International Journal of Physical Distribution and Materials Management,* 10, 1, p. 25.

Figure 25 shows another model which helps put many of these points in context.[6] (The concept behind the model is similar to that of the management theorist Maslow's hierarchy of needs.) The model is based upon the precept that while many factors can influence the buyer to decide one way or another as to any one freight service some factors, because they are more important, need to be satisfied before other factors are even considered.

The factor, or factors, in each level are considered in turn. For example a buyer might be searching for a service to a new export market for his company. He has gone through the various stages implied by Figure 22 and now has some ten services from which he can choose. Each is first appraised

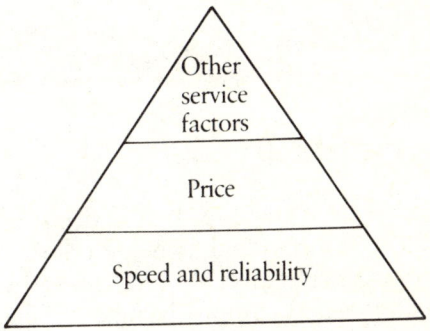

Figure 25   Hierarchy of effects model for freight purchasing.

against the perceived needs for speed and reliability, defined by consultation with export sales and customers and hopefully as a result of an exercise to define the optimum combination of stock levels and delivery service.

Only those services which satisfy the defined criteria are appraised on the next factor, price. Those who meet the price criterion are finally appraised against a selection of other service factors specific to the individual company or buyer.

While Figure 25 is unlikely to represent each purchasing decision with total precision it does describe the way that, an apparent multitude of factors can effect the buying decision while speed, reliability and then price are always paramount.

One example will serve to illustrate the dangers of generalizing on service criteria *always* being more important than price.

A British company involved in the timber trade and in the production of wood products had a successful export market in Scandinavia for wood shavings. Now Scandinavia is one of the world's main production areas for timber. They do nevertheless have a need for wood shavings and chippings to make chipboard products. Their own timber industry cannot always supply enough chippings.

Clearly chippings can be made from timber directly (and not as a by-product) but at a price. The British firm could supply the market cheaper than this price only if they bought freight below a certain price. The level of service was largely irrelevant as the stocks of chippings were normally high.

The dangers of generalization

The decision-making unit

The idea was earlier introduced of a decision-making unit rather than a single individual as being relevant to industrial purchasing decision making. (Figure 26 shows part of the family tree for a typical medium-sized British exporter.) Many individuals may have a say in many freight purchasing decisions. For the sake of simplicity the main part of this chapter referred to a single decision-making role. Many decisions will nevertheless be the prime responsibility of one individual; others will be made by a team.

Those decisions which are normally referred up the management hierarchy include modal switches and other changes of significance. Many freight companies who need to sell a significant change as well as their services (air freight agents trying to attract surface traffic on a TDC analysis argument) may use this idea and avoid contacting the shipping manager and instead sell to his superiors. Similarly the company who knows they are one of a number of approved carriers to a given destination could well concentrate on selling

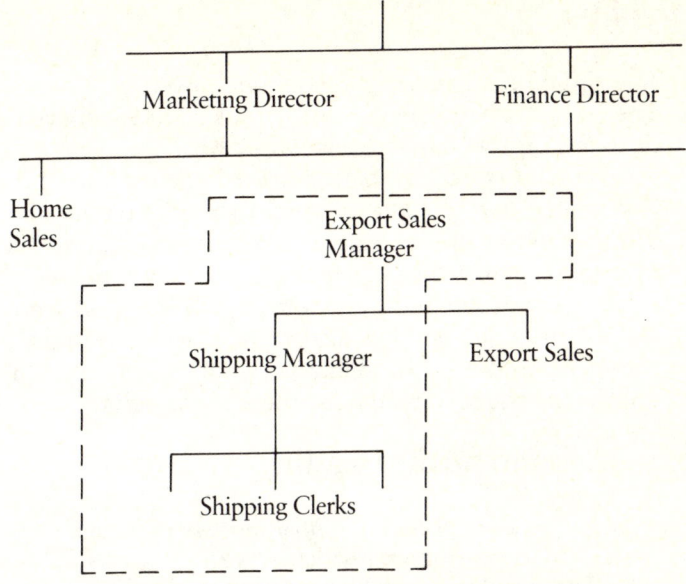

Figure 26 A typical decision-making unit (DMU) for freight.

to the shipping clerk who has the delegated responsibility to choose between approved carriers.

Neither of these tactics should detract from the central role of a professional shipping manager. He is the hub for all freight activities and is rarely irrelevant when freight buying decisions are made. All too often there is no such well-defined role or the person fitting that role is not strong enough to execute it properly.

The central person in any DMU is often referred to as 'the gatekeeper', the person through which information on the purchase decision must pass to reach the organization, and a true shipping manager should fulfil that role. The fact that he is well informed on the freight market, has quantifiable criteria for freight services and is knowledgeable on how each freight service measures against these, makes him the only person capable of making the larger decisions.

All too often the lack of such a systematic approach means others in the organization can impose their opinions on the freight purchase.

Keypoints

1 The shipping manager is a part-time buyer.
2 The complexity of freight buying makes the specification of criteria for a freight service difficult.
3 Service factors are normally more important than price factors in buying freight, especially speed and reliability.
4 The idea of totally rational purchasing in freight is further from reality than the concept of 'subjective rationality'.
5 Despite the problems of quantifying what a good service should provide, purchasing freight can and should be objective in terms of defining what is required and appraising the service against the same criteria.

References and further reading

1 DAVIES, G. J. and GRAY, R. '*Who Buys International Freight Services*' (Maclean Hunter, London, 1979).
2 NEDO, 'Decision Making in Export Shipments', 1974.
3 CIVIL AVIATION AUTHORITY, 'Air Freight Demand', CAP 401, 1977.
4 GRAY, R. 'Modal choice for Urgent Consignments between Britain and Western Europe' in *International Logistics* (MCB, Bradford, 1981).
5 GRAY, R. 'A social-perceptual approach to Freight Transport Modal Choice', PhD Thesis, Cranfield, 1980.
6 GUNTON, C. PhD thesis in preparation, Manchester Polytechnic. *See also* DAVIES, G. and GUNTON, C. 'Marketing International Freight Services' *Quarterly Review of Marketing*, Second Quarter, 1983.

BARKER, D. E. and FARRINGTON, B. *The Basic Arts of Buying* (Business Books Limited, London, 1976).
SLIJPER, MARTIN TH. 'Distribution for Exporters' Management Guide 6, British Institute of Management Foundation, 1977.

8
Freight rates and their negotiation

International freight rates are complex. Rates vary by type of commodity, the ratio of the size to the weight of a consignment and the overall size of the consignment. Most, but not all, companies publish a freight tariff; some of which are regulated nationally or internationally. Unfortunately for the freight buyer few published rates are quoted door-to-door to include all the associated services a trader is likely to require (customs clearance, documentation).

Most freight rates, no matter how formal looking the published tariff might appear, are open to negotiation particularly to the larger buyer. The second half of this chapter is therefore concerned with negotiation skills.

One advantage for the centralized shipping department is the increase in purchasing power it provides. One large exporter funded its centralized service on the discounts in rates it negotiated. Being a large purchaser has other advantages. The company rarely had its goods 'shut out' from a sailing. If too much cargo had been presented for shipment the goods of other companies were left on the quay rather than their own.

Small suppliers or customers realizing the purchasing power of the central department tended to buy on terms which meant they did not arrange freight. This gave the company a price advantage which, on·exports, was used to make a profit by passing on only part of the savings to the customer.

Purchasing power of centralization

Calculating the cube

A carrier has to cover the costs of each journey his vessel, truck or aircraft makes. In all instances there is a limit on the total weight that can be loaded and the space available. The carrier sets his tariff to reflect the fact that a tonne of feathers occupies more space than a tonne of coal but that he can carry a greater volume of the former without exceeding any weight limits.

Carriers charge on the basis of either weight or volume to a given formula. The customer pays whichever yields the higher amount. For example a rate may be £X per tonne or £Y per cubic metre of space whichever yields the higher sum to the carrier.

The volume of a box is easy to define. The rules for calculating the volume of an irregular shape loaded on to a wooden pallet may not be. Normally the dimensions taken ignore the pallet and take the greatest length, breadth and height of the consignment including any projections. Figure 27 demonstrates how even this rule can be less than simple. Based upon a real example $h_2 \times w_2$ yields a different result to $h_1 \times w_1$ – and the article can be stowed either way.

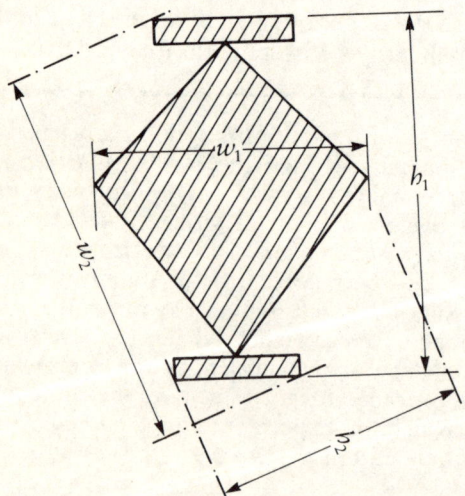

Figure 27 Calculating the freight payable.

The volume and weight tariffs yield the same freight rate at a particular density of freight. This figure is frequently quoted (40 ft^3 per tonne, 1,000 kg per m^3, etc.) to indicate the rate structure.

These ratios rarely persist for all forms of transport. Weight carries a higher premium on airfreight for example. This further complicates the calculation of a total distribution cost to compare surface with air. Lower stocks may mean more smaller consignments but light consignments are sometimes cheaper to move by air than by surface!

Sea freight

Logically freight rates should reflect only the space the consignment occupies, the ease of handling and the availability of capacity. This implies a common rate for most, if not all, commodities. In practice FAK (Freight All Kinds) are rare in ocean freight.

A line or a shipping conference (*see* Chapter 15) will have devised a detailed tariff which rates varying commonly by three-fold between commodities. Shipping lines justify these differences in a number of ways, largely from the value of the cargo. A high freight rate may well discourage a potential exporter of a cheaper and bulkier product while a high rate may be insignificant to an exporter moving small quantities of high value goods.

The growth of containerization has not led to the rationalization of rates to 'box-rates', where a shipper or forwarder pays for the use of a container irrespective of its contents as long as they remain within certain bounds. However the rate structures often include measures to ensure that containers are used to a high capacity. Minimum revenue figures are set per container. Discounts may be offered where a shipper makes good use of a container by careful packing.

Rates for less than full container loads (LCL) are understandably higher than the equivalent full (FCL) rate and in some circumstances it may be cheaper to pay the FCL rate for a partially-filled container.

On most trade routes a Conference of shipping lines offers a common tariff. They also offer an incentive in exchange for an agreement to use the Conference exclusively. This takes the form of a rebate (typically 9–10%) if the shipper abides by the agreement.

The advent of containerization has made it easier for line and shipper to deal directly as the FCL consignment can move readily from door-to-door. The inland movement of the container is frequently governed by a grid tariff whereby, irrespective of the landing or loading point for the container, the shipper pays a haulage rate as if it had arrived at a local port. Lines frequently offer a consolidation or groupage service.

These developments have tended to mean that the forwarder has been by-passed. However the forwarder is still active in even FCL traffic by offering credit on freight, whereas the carrier rarely does so, demanding instead payment prior to shipment or before goods are released to the consignee.

For the larger shipper chartering may be attractive. Charter rates are similar to commodity type rates in that they vary daily. The London Baltic Exchange is a major centre for the arrangement of charters. The advantage for the charterer is that he has full control over the vessel and can frequently negotiate a low rate compared with that from a regular line. The disadvantage is that the charterer can be responsible for the cost of the ship for the whole time taken in the voyage. Very bad weather could mean paying for the vessel while it weathers a storm in a port, at the charterer's expense.

Published liner rates have been subject to two types of surcharge in the 1970s and 1980s. Bunker adjustment factors (baf) and currency adjustment factors (caf) have been used to adjust rates when oil prices have risen or when the dollar (the major unit for quoting rates) has fluctuated in value.

Airfreight rates

Airfreight rates have been determined traditionally by IATA. The original rating structures for air were apparently based on dividing the passenger fare by the notional weight of a typical passenger. Since then the rating structure has become ever more complex although airfreight employs commodity rating less frequently.

Container rates are also available although there is little standardization of air containers. The weight/volume factor in airfreight is 7 m^3 per 1,000 kilo; emphasizing the weight basis of airfreight rates. Most rates are quoted per kilo as a consequence.

The majority of airfreight moves via an airfreight forwarder. The smaller consignments, which dominate airfreight, are generally consolidated into larger units for the carrier. The consolidation savings allow the forwarder to offer a lower rate than the full IATA tariff but the process of consolidation can also delay consignments.

Basically there are two types of airfreight rates, the premium or full IATA rate and the consolidation rate. These have been complicated by the introduction by both carriers and forwarders of other price-service packages.

Many carriers offer cheaper 'deferred' rates where the consignment may not leave on the first available flight but is guaranteed to be moved within a certain time. Forwarders themselves market 'first' and 'second' class services. For small consignments, so called courier services are offered, although a true courier service is unlikely to be possible for other than items with no declarable value such as documents.

In the early 1970s air charter became a significant factor in the airfreight industry. Problems at ports serving the booming oil exporting nations of Africa and the Middle East and those countries' abilities to pay high prices for Western goods encouraged this.

The development of widebodied passenger aircraft, the improvement of port facilities and the slackening of the oil boom has lead to the demise of many charter and all freight operators. Nevertheless charter remains an alternative for the large shipper.

Road haulage rates

Road based rates tend to be less complex than sea or air rates. Depot to depot rates by different weight breaks are generally published. Within certain countries haulage rates are controlled. Additional charges, such as documentation, collection and delivery, and customs clearance are often shown on the rate card enabling the shipper to calculate a door-to-door rate.

In Europe unaccompanied trailers are frequently moved by sea or rail to be picked up by a different driver from the one taking the trailer to the vessel or station. Unaccompanied services, as they are called, are cheaper than accompanied services. The value of the latter is that an experienced driver can negotiate in person with local officials, should the need arise.

The same weight/volume relationships are used to charge for full loads or groupage although most freight will be charged by weight.

A large exporter was concerned about the money it was spending on freight costs. Although much of their traffic was regular it was no easy task to explain to a potential forwarder or carrier how many consignments were moving on what mode at any given time. A detailed schedule was prepared laying out the firm's export distribution business.

The schedule was sent out to a number of forwarders who were invited to tender for the business. Many did. The existing forwarder retained the business although his charges did reduce slightly.

In the following years a similar schedule was issued with the same outcome. The existing company retained the work. The exporter's approach had been successful in forcing down the charges of their existing supplier but at the expense of aggravating other forwarders who felt they had bid lower after spending considerable time on the exporter's complex schedule.

The problems of issuing a freight schedule

Negotiating rates

Many bills for freight exceed the freight rate quoted in the carrier's rate schedule. A closer examination of the invoice may show that a number of extras have been added: surcharges; documentation charges; insurance premiums; customs clearance charges; proof of delivery charge; customs duty; demurrage; and the ubiquitous 'disbursements'. Most, if not all of these, will be perfectly justifiable but mention of these at this stage emphasizes that negotiating rates is not only about negotiating the cost of freight, it is concerned with a portfolio of potential charges. Negotiating only on the basis of a rate can leave open the possibility for the forwarder or carrier to increase his ancillary charges to compensate for any hard-won concessions by the shipper on rates alone.

In recent years considerable progress has been made in formalizing guidelines for successful negotiation, be they rates, wage claims or any other form of discussion between two parties who are exchanging something involving a financial consideration but who are both trying to ensure that they achieve some advantage.

This is the essence of negotiation. First there must be, at least, the probability of an agreement. Secondly the cost or price of what is being exchanged is only one element open for discussion and agreement. Despite the advances made in understanding negotiating technique, negotiation remains an art. A manager's skills can be enhanced but a basic negotiating ability is difficult to learn. Negotiation can be divided into three parts: preparation; negotiating itself; summarizing and concluding.

Figure 28 offers a checklist for the first stage: preparation. It is unreasonable to expect any manager to perform well if he hurries into a complex negotiation with no preparation and possibly straight from dealing with other matters which have dominated his thinking.

One of the best researched studies on negotiating comes from the Huthwaite Research Group. They analysed the behaviour of managers, trade unionists and others who were involved in a variety of negotiating. They looked at two groups, those regarded by their peers as successful negotiators and others who were classified as average negotiators. Their work confirms the importance of preparation but also stresses the quality of that preparation. Average negotiators were found to explore only half the possible options or outcomes in their preparation. The skilled concentrated on areas of potential agreement. Average negotiators tended to concentrate in their planning on short-term issues.

1 Have they the capacity (at least on paper) to undertake the work under consideration?
2 Does their representative have the power/authority to negotiate or will many points have to be confirmed?
3 What criteria, other than price, need to be defined?
4 What factors other than the freight rate will be charged for?
5 What is the maximum price/minimum level of service we can accept?
6 What price/service levels would we reasonably expect to settle for?
7 What is the best deal we could possibly expect to negotiate?
8 Where are negotiations to be held? Is the environment to our advantage?
9 Do we negotiate as a team? If so, does each member of the team know his role?
10 What points/factors are they likely to raise? What is our response to each?
11 What data can be uncovered about them to aid our negotiating position?

Figure 28   Checklist for negotiation: preparation.

This last point is relevant to point seven in Figure 28. It is possible to be too skilled at negotiating rates and get agreement to what amounts to uneconomic rates. The forwarder or carrier may well fail financially if the contract is large enough with undesirable consequences for the shipper.

The skilled negotiator rarely has a single, inflexible rate for which to aim. He establishes a range he can settle within and uses other secondary factors to trade off against the main rates being negotiated.

One final point from the Huthwaite research. Skilled negotiators do not tend to evolve a negotiating plan or schedule. They are more likely to keep an open mind on the sequence of issues.

The message on planning negotiations is to plan but plan flexibly. Much time might be wasted in considering factors which never arise but enough of relevance will have been achieved to ensure a satisfactory negotiation.

---

1 Question the other side. Probe for the main points they consider important. Get all the issues on to the table for discussion
2 Constantly re-emphasize areas of agreement.
3 Do not use too many supporting arguments.
4 Avoid quantifying your position first on the major issues.
5 Be prepared to trade off price and non-price factors.
6 Finish the negotiating session with a summary of all points of agreement.

Figure 29   Checklist for negotiation: negotiating.

Figure 29 offers a checklist for the negotiations themselves. The more important the contract the more protracted will be the face-to-face sessions. Frequently the first side to quantify their position (we consider £X per tonne the only possible rate) find themselves at a disadvantage if the other side respond with a qualitative reply (£X per tonne is totally uneconomic you'll have to offer better than that).

Perhaps the most important findings from the Huthwaite research concern the relative time spent asking questions. Skilled negotiators spend nearly a quarter of their time asking questions compared with the 10% spent by the average negotiator. The skilled man is often trying to establish or emphasize those areas where agreement has been, or seems to have been, reached.

A mistake in negotiation apparently is to make too many points in support of one's argument. This offers the other side more opportunity to knock the argument down. An essential part of negotiation is to restate the points of agreement once every issue has been decided. In the euphoria of having reached what appears to be a good conclusion the different parties may leave with small but significant differences in their understandings of what has been agreed.

Keypoints

1 Freight rates are complex. It is difficult to calculate a door-to-door rate in advance.

2 Freight tariffs are rarely non-negotiable in practice. The rate itself is only one element. Ancillary service costs should be negotiated simultaneously.

3 Ground rules for negotiation are being defined to enable the negotiator to improve his techniques.

9
Packing and packaging

This chapter is concerned with the additional challenges posed in the area of packing and packaging because a good is exported. It has been estimated that 2% of carrier revenue goes in meeting claims for loss or damage of goods entrusted to their care. In a Manchester Polytechnic survey of shippers in Britain, France and Germany, 11 of 143 respondents estimated that export packing added more than 20% to the weight of their goods.[1] Many exporters, it seems, choose to, or have to, resort to large expenditure on packing but, despite this, loss and damage remains a significant factor.

Export packing is a specialist area in its own right. In Britain a full apprenticeship is still served to become a qualified case maker, traditionally the main method of packing using a wooden crate. Perhaps as a consequence, in the survey mentioned earlier, although all respondents were responsible for shipping, less than half were responsible for export packing. Production or a separate despatch department were most frequently the responsible area. The involvement of production is quite logical where the company has adopted the 'unit load' concept (*see* below) where the production unit, storage unit and even the unit of sale are identical.

Goods require packaging for many reasons, the most obvious being to contain the product. New materials, the demands of the market place for more aesthetic and eye-catching presentation have combined to form the basis of a separate business function within many firms. Where this function exists it may be preferable for the specialist to extend his responsibility to the problems of export rather than add to the shipping manager's role. Packing does nevertheless remain an integral part of the logistics process.

Among the facets of packaging, more relevant to export, are loss (from misdirection or pilferage), damage (climatic, physical, contamination) and the provision of handling points for a range of transport types and levels of sophistication of both equipment and labour.

A leading American confectionery manufacturer was concerned about the high level of cracking in the chocolate-coated products exported from one of its European factories to Switzerland. The damage was not apparent in an identical product sold throughout Europe. It did not appear to be associated with rough handling, since other similar products were unaffected. Neither did the damage appear limited to a particular consignment, although the problem had only recently been noted. The customer blamed the quality of the packing material. After an expensive investigation, including the analysis of packaging materials, the problem was isolated to a change in the way the confectionery had been transported. A new route had meant the goods were carried over a high mountain pass, high enough to lower the external air pressure sufficiently for the chocolate-coated product to burst. Different climatic conditions are not limited to differences in temperature or humidity.

Detective work in product damage

The issue of loss is better left to a later discussion on containerization and shipping marks. First the problem of damage.

An export consignment is likely to be handled many times. Its journey time is likely to be long. It may reside in a warehouse or in the open at the quayside or in the middle of a Siberian field next to a new chemical plant. The packing should eliminate the more obvious points of damage from mechanical handling. However, good packing also means stopping damage such as abrasion between the product and the packing material.

International movements are normally made in larger vessels than for national delivery. Goods from other companies are more likely to be stowed nearby and for longer periods. The dangers of contamination from chemical odours is higher, tainting foodstuffs or corroding machinery. Damaged goods can be repaired or replaced more easily on a home order. The problem of damage normally implies higher cost, higher quality packing.

A minority of exporters handle their own case-making. Most use specialist packers. They have to balance the danger of damage against both the cost of the packing and the increase in freight costs incurred by increasing the consignments' weight and/or volume.

One exporter was concerned about the large bills he received from his export packer. The company in question had a good reputation but was the only packer for many miles. Overseas customers had complained about the quantity of timber used in the case-making which made cases more difficult to dismantle than those from other suppliers. Examining the work done by the packer suggested that he was charging an appropriate rate for the work done but that too much packing was being used.

A visit to the packer provided an answer. The firm had recently instituted a bonus scheme designed to encourage greater productivity. The bonus was paid on the length of timber used per day. This encouraged greater output but also encouraged the overuse of timber.

Checking packing charges

Some markets, notably the USSR, are particularly sensitive about the quality of packing. They tend to specify fairly precisely how consignments are to be packed and issue a list of approved packers from whom the exporter has to choose. In the survey mentioned earlier the majority of exporters received packing specifications which they considered to be non-standard from customers.

One point which is rarely mentioned in the context of packing industrial goods, although it is always mentioned for consumer products, is the aesthetic appeal of packaging. A distant importer's first sight of his purchase is the packing not the product. Skimpy packing poorly executed may save money but there can be a consequent loss in customer confidence in the care he thinks the exporter takes.

Few exports are sold ex-works unpacked (although Incoterms are a little vague on precisely how much packing an ex-works price should include). Even an ex-works sale places an onus on the exporter to ensure that his goods arrive in reasonable condition.

Defining the quality of packing to guard against physical rather than environmental damage is difficult. One company devised a pragmatic test which, while it had no basis in the theory of strength of materials, was at least an objective attempt to assess the company's packing.

Packed product was thrown from one person to another down a flight of steps a given number of times. It was then rolled down the same flight of steps. The boxes were unwrapped and any damage assessed. Packing allowing 90% of undamaged product was considered acceptable.

No packing can guarantee zero damage. Not all packages will be subject to impact likely to cause damage. But tests like these provide some guidance on the quality of packaging. If used in conjunction with checks at the receiving end of the distribution pipeline then the packaging scientist and distribution manager are better placed to judge the quality of their packing.

Judging the quality of packing

Packing materials have changed over the years. The dominance of wood has declined as cheaper alternatives have evolved and the unit load and through movement concepts have reduced the need for high quality packing.

Plywood, lighter and less bulky for the same strength, has replaced wood in part. Fibreboard and cardboard cartons are more than adequate for many products and markets. Some markets place restrictions on packing materials including material used to fill in between a packed unit and its crate. Wool, straw and other organic materials should be checked for acceptability before use.

Unitization

The concept of unitization can be defined in a number of ways. Essentially it recognizes the economies possible by grouping product units together and handling these multi-units rather than individual units.

A pallet containing six drums or twenty boxes is easier to move than six or twenty separate items. Clearly moving a loaded pallet requires some mechanical aid. Unitization offers labour savings at the expense of investment in unit load devices and handling equipment. Nevertheless savings of around 20% are quoted in distribution costs from adopting the idea.

The pallet is the most common unit load device but its use has been partially replaced by skids (flat sheets) or methods of disposing entirely with a pallet called 'non-pallet palletizing'. Here shrink wrap or stretch wrap holds sacks or bags of material in a shape allowing access to the forks on a fork-lift truck.

These methods can be of monetary value to the exporter in many ways. Shipping lines often offer discounts for unitized cargo. Quicker, safer handling reduces the loading time on a vessel and can aid storage. Containers, themselves a unit load device, should be 'stuffed' as fully as possible to take full advantage of the space, within the limit on weight. Palletized goods may be easy to move in and out of a container but pallets themselves occupy valuable space. Skids or non-pallet palletizing allow better usage at the expense of a slightly increased chance of damage.

Not all cargo can be unitized. One analysis shows current and projected volumes of British trade by handling category

(Table 3). The gradual growth in unitizable cargo is still insufficient to make it the dominant method of shipment. However, for manufactured and semi-manufactured goods with which this book is mainly concerned, unitization is important.

Table 3
UK non-fuel foreign trade by cargo type 1971–88. From Fenyoe, R. and Tonkin, N. 'Forecasting Foreign Trade', *International Journal of Physical Distribution*, Vol. 11, 5/6 (1981) p. 85.

	1971	1978	1983	1988
Bulk	47	43	42	40
Semi-bulk	27	29	27	27
Unitizable	26	28	31	33

The full advantages of the unit load come from making the unit compatible with production, warehousing, distribution and marketing. Ideally the customer should be buying in the most economic units, i.e. in container or pallet loads.

Containerization

The modern container has its origins in America during the 1930s. By the 1950s, encouraged by their use during the Second World War, containership operations became a reality. Standards for containers were drawn up early in the 1960s which led the way for the harmonization of equipment so necessary to make full use of the concept. It remains one of the few truly international standards quoted in Imperial measurements with the standard being 20 foot and 40 foot containers. Most statistics on the industry are quoted in 20 foot equivalents.

The important dimensions on a container to the carrier are its external length and width. There is some variation possible in height. The International Standards Organization (ISO) has defined the standard sizes. Within this framework a number of variants have evolved (Figure 30).

Containers can move directly from consignor to consignee via a number of transport modes. The large (and heavy) containers are not compatible with airfreight although some

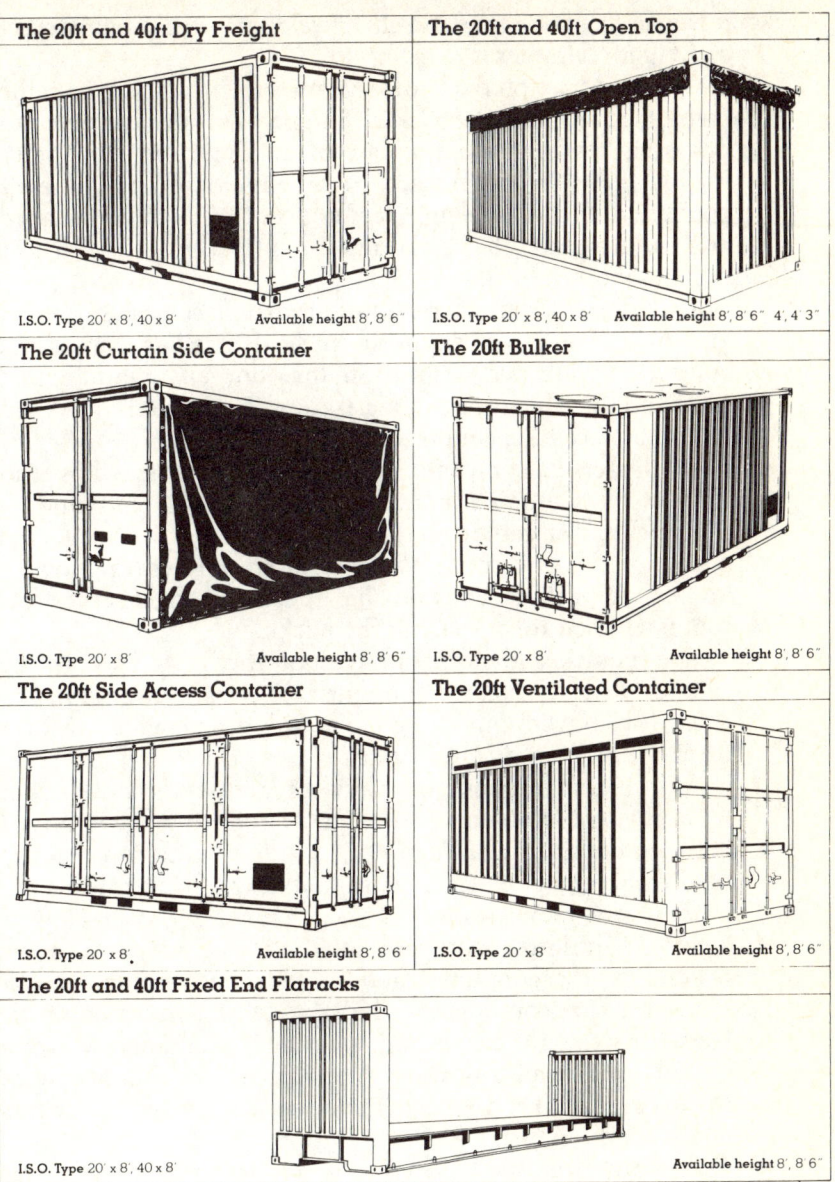

The 20ft and 40ft Dry Freight

I.S.O. Type 20' x 8', 40 x 8' Available height 8', 8' 6"

The 20ft and 40ft Open Top

I.S.O. Type 20' x 8', 40 x 8' Available height 8', 8' 6" 4', 4' 3'

The 20ft Curtain Side Container

I.S.O. Type 20' x 8' Available height 8', 8' 6"

The 20ft Bulker

I.S.O. Type 20' x 8' Available height 8', 8' 6"

The 20ft Side Access Container

I.S.O. Type 20' x 8' Available height 8', 8' 6"

The 20ft Ventilated Container

I.S.O. Type 20' x 8' Available height 8', 8' 6"

The 20ft and 40ft Fixed End Flatracks

I.S.O. Type 20' x 8', 40 x 8' Available height 8', 8' 6"

Figure 30   Different containers (courtesy of Adamson Containers Ltd).

advance has been made in the development of a lightweight airfreight container.

Containerization requires large investment – not only in the containers or boxes themselves. Shippers may need to redesign despatch bays to accommodate them. Container ships with their cellular structure need to be built or existing vessels converted. Handling equipment at ports needs to be installed and understandable trade union antipathy overcome as manual jobs are lost.

Thus the concept has spread somewhat piecemeal, one trade at a time. The initial euphoria in the 1970s has evaporated somewhat with the realization that not all manufactured goods are suitable for containerization. New vessels now tend to combine cellular and traditional holds.

Containers have meant greater speed. Container ships tend to be faster. Container handling reduces loading and unloading times by a sizeable order. Damage rates are lower. Pilferage is reduced. As a consequence insurance rates are lower. Immediate packing does not have to be as strong since the container itself forms part of the packing.

The financial advantages have not always accrued to the shipper. Freight rates on containerized services are similar to those for conventional cargo. The shipper benefits however from the decreased transit time.

A problem with container services, and with many freight services, is the imbalance of cargo in both tonnage and type between destinations. The imports into a developed country tend to be higher in tonnage than its exports and to consist more of raw materials.

Some solutions to this problem lie in the adaption of the product to the container mode. Other innovations make it easier to utilize containers for bulk products. Rubber or plastic bags for example can be hung inside a container allowing granular material or powder to be shipped without problems of leakage or dirtying a container used for manufactured goods on the return leg.

Containerization of a trade may not be in the best interests of the shipper whose goods do not fit economically into a container. White goods (washing machines, cookers, etc.) are regular in shape, fairly square and bulky. One company manufacturing such products made considerable savings by reducing one dimension on their products by about 1 cm. The packed goods could be loaded far better into a container.

Despite the ISO standardization of container sizes, containers do vary in their internal dimensions. A precise calculation of loading may be rendered redundant by such variations. Pallet sizes may not be totally compatible with container dimensions. Even the ISO pallet sizes do not load economically into an ISO container.

Adopting the unit load concept is then no guarantee of economy. It requires research to define the best approach.

Future trends

The growth in containerization has already slowed but it will continue as more trades are containerized and more products are made compatible with the container. Materials used in immediate packing and case making are likely to change. Ecologists are concerned about the dwindling resources of certain materials and the price of timber has risen substantially while the quality of softwoods is said to have fallen. More pressure on the reuse of packing materials can therefore be expected.

Some products, such as natural and man-made fibres, are distributed and sold in bales. Such products are often fairly light and attract freight rates based on volume rather than weight. There is therefore potential to produce denser bales and save on transport costs.

An executive from a leading man-made fibre company complained that the company had not taken account of the relationship between bale density and shipping costs and therefore final selling price. Installing heavy, and more expensive, baling machines could reduce the bale size substantially. Not only would this have reduced freight costs it would have reduced freight costs sufficiently to allow the company to compete with supplies from other countries in distant markets thus opening up business potential otherwise denied to them.

Investment in baling equipment opens up new markets

A British pharmaceutical company exported its products world-wide. In some markets certain products had only a limited sale. In these markets labelling requirements were often quite extensive. In one example the manufacturer's name, their agent's name and other information had to appear on the product label in the native language.

The company solved the problem of non-standard labelling, not by holding stock of each variant, but by holding limited stock of unlabelled product. This stock was labelled when an order was received in an expensive, labour-intensive, special department. On balance this was cheaper than holding stock of every minor variant labelled on the production line.

Dealing with special packs

Shipping marks and labelling

Each export consignment needs to be identifiable to aid its movement, to ensure products are carried in safety, and to reduce the risk of loss. Shipping marks serve these functions.

A basic problem is to use a marking system which is simple but which can be readily understood by people of different nationalities. There are other points that need remembering which include security, making sure high value products are not easily identifiable to a potential thief, and indicating to people handling goods that they need to be stowed in a certain way or handled with especial care.

In 1979 a Working Party under the United Nations presented certain ideas on the simplification of shipping marks. They proposed that a mark could contain little more than an abbreviated form of the consignee's name, an order number, the destination and a code identifying the package if it was one of a series.

Figure 31 illustrates a typical simple shipping mark.

X Y Z	(Consignee)
92 / B	(Reference number)
FREEMANTLE	(Destination)
2 / 10	(Package number)

The consignee is the X Y Z company under contract number 92 / B to be consigned to Freemantle and the package is the second of ten.

Figure 31   A simple shipping mark and its meaning.

Other information may be necessary on the outside of the package but this can be added separately as one or more standard stickers indicating hazardous goods, fragile goods, and so on. Further information may be felt necessary on the outside of the package. This can be provided separately perhaps as a typed document attached to the side of the case.

The case mark may have to appear on documentation relating to the consignment. It may have to comply with a letter of credit. Frequently the mark has to be in a foreign language or in a different script from Roman. Accuracy is therefore important.

As has been pointed out earlier the shipping manager is not always responsible for packing. He does however need to ensure that communications on case marking are precise. One method mentioned earlier is to use a series of codes between the two departments. Thus shipping mark 123/A would refer to the mark normally used for a regular customer whose goods are labelled in English and Arabic.

Keypoints

1   Export packing is not always the direct responsibility of the shipping manager but it is certainly part of the logistics process.

2 Packing costs need to be balanced against loss and damage rates and against the impression good presentation makes on a customer.

3 Packing methods and materials are constantly evolving and need monitoring to ensure the most effective methods and materials are being used.

4 Unitization is a money-saving concept which is very relevant to the exporter/importer.

5 Containerization was the main unit load revolution in the liner trades in the 1960s and 1970s. Further growth is expected.

6 Shipping marks need not be complex but must be precise.

References and further reading

1 GUMBRELL, K. A. PhD thesis, (Manchester Polytechnic, 1983).

DEPARTMENT OF INDUSTRY *Packing for Profit* (HMSO, London, 1979).

DEPARTMENT OF INDUSTRY *Pallet Usage and Wastage* (HMSO, London, 1977).

SITPRO *Simpler Shipping Marks* (London, 1981).

10
The importer's perspective

Every export is someone else's import. Very few international consignments are deal with entirely by either the consignee or the consignor. In airfreight, for example, decisions on whether to use the mode for a particular consignment are divided equally between the two.

While earlier chapters have tended either to mention the importer in passing while concentrating on international distribution from the exporter's point of view, this chapter includes a number of points which are best examined from the importer's perspective.

Most developed economies import greater tonnages than they export. The trade imbalance can be of the order of two to one. Potentially the importer is badly placed to negotiate freight rates if the carrier cannot rely upon a return load. This is particularly relevant to commodities requiring specialized equipment or vessels, for example foodstuffs needing refrigeration or bulk raw materials such as crude oil.

The imbalance in trade volumes and the mismatch of capacity imply yet another problem for the average importer in a developed nation. Raw materials will be cheaper than manufactured goods and freight costs will therefore form a higher proportion of total expenditure. This link between purchasing for the firm's manufacturing processes and international freight is relevant to the issue of who controls import freight; the shipping department or the purchasing department?

In a survey of British shipping managers[1] 25% did not

devote any time to import shipping and 85% devoted less than 25% of their time to this area. By contrast only 3.4% devoted no time to export shipping and only 25% less than 25% of their time to this area.

There are two explanations for this, apart from the company not importing at all, first that imports are more likely to be controlled by a separate purchasing department and, secondly, that many companies leave control over imports either to their consignors or to wholesalers and other middle men from whom they buy as if the goods were available domestically.

The advantage for a purchasing department to control freight on imports lies in the need to co-ordinate the timing of purchases arriving in the firm with the manufacturing process. The potential disadvantages in this arrangement are the need to duplicate expertise and the probable loss in opportunity to negotiate discounts from the larger purchasing potential of a combined function.

The temptation for the purchasing department must be to buy on a delivered price basis while a professional shipping manager may be more willing to arrange freight on an ex-works purchase with a potential saving on freight.

Clearly the second approach is more compatible with the concept of international logistics. The more relevant issue is whether the company concerned is buying from a supplier better placed than he to obtain low freight rates and the best service.

On many commodity and raw material purchases the selling company will be better placed to control freight. The same goods are likely to be used by many different companies whose orders can be combined to obtain bulk freight rates to a suitable point to break bulk.

Many companies rely heavily upon import efficiency, for example, a wine merchant or a furniture manufacturer importing timber. The logic of combining a purchasing and shipping function is therefore quite strong in such companies.

Japanese companies refer to a management concept called Kanban in the context of purchasing and distribution management. Stated simply, Kanban is to buy just the right amount of material at just the right time.

Two costs are being manipulated, the cost of holding large stocks is being minimized and the cost penalty of stopping the manufacturing process, because there is no raw material, being avoided.

Clearly this concept does not save everyone money. Supplier companies may not find it economic to supply in quantities more suited to their customers' production needs and may also have to incur the cost of holding buffer stocks themselves. The concept may well result in having to pay higher prices for supplies. Nevertheless the overall cost to the buying company may well be much lower.

In the same way that selling companies can analyse historical demand patterns to calculate an optimum size for stocks of finished goods to meet all but an extraordinary sales request, so manufacturers can analyse their production requirements to ensure that only an appropriate level of material is bought.

KANBAN: The Japanese approach to procurement

Customs clearance

All importers share one problem, that of customs clearance. Governments and their agencies are understandably less concerned with scrutinizing exports than they are with imports. Import control is not only concerned with import tariffs and quotas but it is also concerned with the collection of national and local taxes, such as Value Added Tax or state taxes.

Import procedures consist of two components, assessing the goods and their associated documentation as to the value of the goods and whether the goods are subject to any restriction. Any doubts on either will result in goods' being put to one side for further scrutiny.

Assuming that the vast majority of traders are not concerned with evading quotas, tariffs or taxes, they have to concern themselves with the accuracy of documentation and the completeness of the information they provide to both officialdom and forwarders and carriers.

Custom's procedures vary around the world and are likely to change frequently. Many customs processes are becoming computerized. Cargo manifests are presented to customs who choose whether to inspect documentation, goods, both or neither. In the last instance the goods are ready for despatch.

Certain types of goods are liable to more rigorous inspection than others – for example agricultural produce shipped into America. Other inspection procedures appear to be more random, with very thorough checks being instituted occasionally to discourage the dishonest trader or smuggler. Delays to goods in transit are therefore unavoidable due to random Customs checks but the likelihood of delay can be minimized by exporter, importer, forwarder and carrier providing perfect data on documentation.

In their efforts to protect their domestic manufacturing base, governments have been known to put barriers in the way of imported goods, or at least they have been slow to remove laws or regulations which are known to hinder the free trade of goods.

National laws or regulations can also be used to hinder the import of goods particularly if they are not applied so rigorously to the locally produced equivalents.

Two examples illustrate the possibilities.

A French company wished to market a new control device for domestic showers. Another European country had no similar product available for sale. Competitive products were either much more expensive or not as accurate. The importing country's national law required that all plumbing fittings be approved by a water authority. Tests were normally carried out promptly. These particular devices were put on test for well over a year, by which time a domestic firm had developed and was marketing a similar product (which had apparently passed its test in a matter of weeks).

In 1982 the French Government suddenly announced that certain categories of goods, including highly popular video recorders imported from Japan, could only be imported through a limited number of customs points. Goods were delayed as a result and the move was seen as an attempt to limit the import of the specified goods.

Delaying imports

A major tax in many countries is VAT, Value Added Tax. This can range from as low as 4 to 5% on certain goods in certain countries to figures of nearer 30% of their sales value.

Some freight companies will undertake to pay VAT on imports on behalf of their clients. Others have arrangements with customs whereby the company guarantees that the correct amount of VAT will be paid at a future date. Either system allows goods to be delivered quickly rather than wait for the necessary payments to be made.

However in many cases the importer's VAT number needs to be known before the goods can be cleared. In Britain alone there are about 1.5 million VAT registered businesses and a major problem exists on imports to casual traders in identifying their VAT numbers, possibly out of office hours, to allow goods to continue on their journey.

The author was once telephoned late one evening by a freight company with whom he was working at the time to see whether he could discover the VAT number of a small local firm. The import consignment was urgent but was not going to move without a VAT number, a piece of information which the consignor and consignee had failed to provide.

Providing data on imports

The importer is as much a part of the logistics process as the exporter, forwarder and carrier. When considering this as a business system what matters is who is in control, exporter or importer. Frequently the importer will undertake some responsibility for part of the process even if he is buying on delivered terms. He may well insist on consignment via his own clearance agent. Breaking the door-to-door system in this way can be advantageous in some circumstances, where for example the market is distant from the exporter and local knowledge in the importer's country is paramount. However all too many international consignments are delayed because of a break in the door-to-door chain as control is passed from one party to another midway in the transit. Tradition plays its part with traders being reluctant to deviate from established terms of sale and include responsibility for customs and local taxes, even in highly integrated markets such as the EEC.

As is pointed out in the next chapter, control over the through movement is a more relevant concept than whether a term of sale is delivered or ex-works. Whatever the terms of sale and whoever controls freight, the importer is examining the system from a more critical perspective than the exporter.

The exporter is concerned with seeing his goods on their way. The importer is concerned with seeing them arrive as arranged. The exporter is well advised to view the logistics process from his customer's perspective from time to time. After all, satisfying his needs is the source of the exporter's profit, not ensuring that goods are effectively despatched.

Keypoints

1 The importer can be the major decision maker on an export consignment.
2 Import and export shipping are not always a combined function in trading companies.
3 Import management are particularly concerned with problems of customs clearance. Such problems are associated with information accuracy and attempts to impose non-tariff barriers to imports.
4 Adopting the importer's perspective can be a valuable exercise for the exporter.

References and further reading

1   DAVIES, G. J. and GRAY, R. *Who Buys International Freight Services* (Maclean Hunter, London 1980).

11
Terms of trade

Terms of trade are used to define both the instance where the responsibility for control over the movement of goods between exporter and importer occurs and who is responsible for which cost element during the transfer of goods. Differences in language, usage and legal system between countries prompted the International Chamber of Commerce to codify the main terms of international trade in 1936 with the first publication of 'Incoterms'. This remains, in its updated form, the only internationally recognized source of definition for, not only the meaning of terms such as FOB or CIF but also, the detail on the relative responsibilities of exporter and importer.

Unfortunately Incoterms are not universally accepted nor are they, with certain exceptions, legally binding. The USA, for example, has not employed Incoterms as a convention preferring its own hybrid terms 'the revised American Foreign Trade Definitions 1941'. However the major terms, to which this chapter limits itself, are common to both systems and the USA is now adopting the international standard in many cases.

Basically terms of trade extend from the position where the exporter has to do little, if anything, more than make his goods available to the importer or his agent at the factory gate (ex-works, ex-factory, etc.) to the position where the exporter undertakes to deliver his goods free of any administrative problems into the hands of his customer at his own factory gate (free delivered, franco-domicile, etc.).

Ex-works, ex-factory	Minimal responsibility for the seller.
FOB, FOT, FOR	Free on board, free on truck, free on rail. The exporter bears the costs up to the point where the goods have been loaded on to the mode of (normally) international carriage. It is usual for these terms to be qualified in some way.
CIF	Cost, Insurance and Freight. The most common 'delivered' term on deep sea traffic where the exporters' responsibilities largely end at the agreed point of discharge.
Delivered, free delivered, franco domicile	Maximum responsibility for the seller.

Figure 32   Common terms of trade.

Terms of trade can be regarded as additive. For example a CIF sale includes the responsibilities to FOB and an FOB sale includes the responsibilities to ex-works (Figure 32). At each stage one party passes over more responsibility to the other.

The advantages of delivered pricing

In some circumstances it is clearly essential for an exporter to sell ex-works, for example where his goods are being consolidated with those of another company as part of a major export shipment against a jointly negotiated contract. In general exporters are encouraged to sell delivered. Ex-works or FOB pricing on exports is decried as lazy or as plain bad marketing. The customer, it is said, wants a delivered price, in his own currency to compare with locally available alternatives.

There are other advantages to delivered pricing. An exporter selling delivered is more likely to specify the services of a carrier of his own nationality. Delivered pricing could well be therefore in the national interest and make a contribution to a country's balance of payments. Government bodies are consequently to be seen promoting the idea of delivered pricing, supported by their national transport lobby.

A more direct advantage to the exporter is where he is selling through a local agent. The exporter knows, or should know, the local price for similar goods. However if he sells ex-works he has no knowledge of the detailed breakdown of the contribution made by the various costs between ex-works and the local selling price of his goods. His foreign agent will tend to tell him the ex-works price 'necessary' to compete in the foreign market after freight, taxes, warehousing, etc. are taken into consideration. How much commission the agent seeks to make may be unclear even from his own detailed breakdown of costs. The closer to a delivered price the exporter sells the closer he will be to controlling the intermediate costs to his, rather than to his agent's, advantage.

The case for delivered pricing appears clear. Why then are those exporters who sell ex-works or FOB losing out? The answer is that there are almost as many valid reasons for selling ex-works or FOB.

In many trades it is the custom of that trade to sell ex-works or FOB. The British china industry, and the French Cognac industry are two of the more successful product groups in world trade. Both, by custom, sell FOB. Whether one company in either sector could gain advantage from selling delivered is unproven but all seem to agree by their actions that it is not in their best interests to break ranks.

A number of British companies sell on the basis of FOB plus services. In other words their price lists are in FOB terms but the importer is normally provided with a delivered price. The exporter does not have the problem of maintaining a multitude of price lists for all markets as the same FOB list suffices for all.

The issue of pricing exports on FOB or delivered terms is more critical when the order processing system is computerized. The FOB price list can be held as relatively static data but delivered prices can only be maintained if freight forms a small part of the delivered price or the company has only a few, stable export clients. The cost of freight is sometimes added manually or via the computer system to a computer printed invoice if the cost is known at the time of despatch. So few freight rates are quoted door-to-door that the final bill may not be known until after delivery.

Delivered pricing and computer systems

There may well be legal advantages in pricing at FOB plus services rather than CIF. Technically the exporter is arranging freight as the importer's agent in an FOB plus services contract. It may be reasonable to add a handling charge to the freight account to make freight more of a profit than a cost centre.

Other reasons for not adopting delivered pricing include transfer pricing between two units of the same multinational company and where a small firm is selling to a much larger firm with better purchasing power on freight. Both can be criticized. Why for example should a transfer price be ex-works rather than delivered? Why should a large firm invariably obtain better rates on a consignment merely because they are large when other factors such as imbalances in capacity or fluctuations in currencies between markets can mean that an exporter can sometimes buy the same capacity far cheaper than the importer?

The issue of delivered pricing has been clarified by a survey by Keith Gumbrell of the Manchester Polytechnic, sponsored by *International Freighting Management*.[1] The main results of a combined questionnaire and interview survey of 97 British companies are presented in Figure 33.

The interviewees in each case were the managers responsible for international distribution (shipping managers). While they are responsible for arranging the details of their company's freight they were not necessarily even consulted on the terms their organization sells on. A sub-sample of 47 (those contacted personally) were asked whether they were ever consulted on terms of trade decisions. 27 said yes and 20 no. The 56 contacted by postal questionnaire were asked about the frequency of any consultation. Only 9 were always consulted, 24 usually consulted, 21 sometimes and 4 never consulted.

The lack of consultation between sales and shipping gave rise to certain anomalies. In one instance a company's sales department had agreed a 'freight forward' contract to a market which did not accept such contracts. In another, the same client had been traded with on three different sets of terms, over a short period of time.

The survey asked questions on the number of export consignments and their value so that the responses of each company could be weighted to provide a better overview of all British trade. The pattern for Figure 33 (*a–c*) is, however, fairly consistent. Slightly under half of British exports at the time were sold up to FOB and slightly more on what amount to delivered terms. Respondents were asked whether they would, given a free choice (presumably by both their firm and the customer) continue to sell on current terms. Nearly half said they would not.

The pattern for preferred export terms in Figure 33(*e*) is not too dissimilar from the pattern of most often used terms in Figure 33(*c*) with a small increase in the proportion of delivered terms. The small change does however disguise a significant trend. Of the 47 shippers who were dissatisfied with their company's current terms, 27 wanted to see an increase in control, i.e. more delivered terms, and 20 wanted less control, i.e. terms closer to ex-works. Interestingly the shippers who had earlier said that they were not consulted on terms of trade were much more likely to want more control over delivery.

A fair test of whether companies do, or do not, want delivered terms is to examine the terms on which they sell as well as those on which they buy. If companies generally want a delivered price this should be revealed by comparing what terms companies buy and sell on. Figure 33(*f*) and (*g*) are the results for the same firms as surveyed on export terms, this time on import terms.

Not surprisingly, as we are now dealing with only one customer, there was less of a spread in the responses from individual companies. Ten firms for example always bought

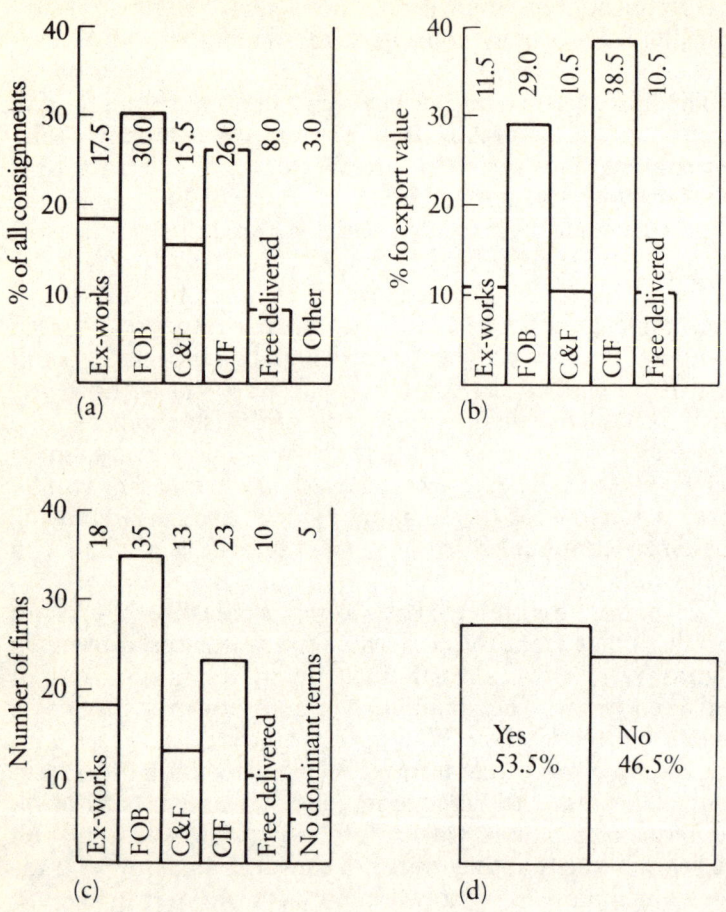

Figure 33 Terms of trade of British companies. (*a*) Terms of export trade by number of consignments; (*b*) terms of export trade, value weighted ('other' excluded); (*c*) most often used export terms; (*d*) 'Would you sell under your current usual terms; (*e*) preferred export terms (includes multiple replies); (*f*) terms of import purchase by number of consignments; (*g*) most often used import terms (65 firms).

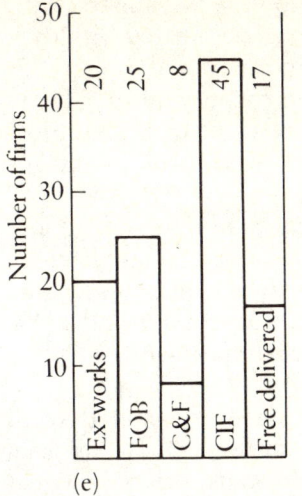

(e)

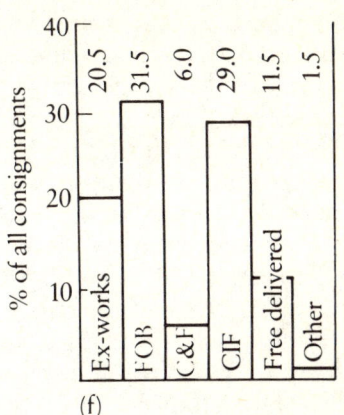

(f)

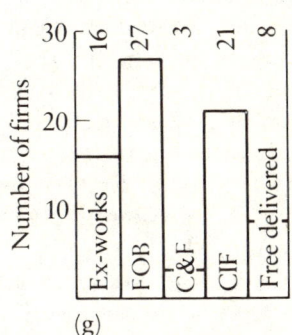

(g)

Figure 33   *(cont.)*

on the same terms. Over half the companies used one set of terms for at least 75% of all their import consignments.

Respondents were more satisfied with their predominant terms of import, 44 of the 65 who were concerned with imports were satisfied with their current usual terms. Of those who were dissatisfied, 8 wanted more control over freight themselves, i.e. less delivered terms, and 13 wanted less control.

The histograms of import terms look very similar to the export terms, with fewer shippers being dissatisfied with their company's terms of purchase on international trade. The implication is that companies do not, by any means, always want to buy delivered and when they want to change their terms they do not invariably move to less control on imports and more control on exports.

A better description of the significance of terms of trade is that companies appear to want to control the freight element or not. A company who does not want to control freight selling to a company who does is in a perfectly acceptable and stable relationship and is providing the customer with what he wants, an ex-works or FOB price.

It follows that the typical exporter has to be prepared to sell on a variety of terms if he wishes to confine himself to offering what the customer wants. To offer delivered terms only would mean imposing the same on the buyer who wants control over freight.

The same survey was repeated on French and German firms. The way companies manage export distribution in both countries differs somewhat from that in Britain. The shipping manager's role is a very rare role indeed in both countries. Export distribution tends to be handled by a sales-orientated manager or by a domestic transport manager. The differences are partly a result of French firms being smaller than their British counterparts and partly from Britain's greater involvement in world rather than just European markets.

Table 4 presents part of the results of the French and German survey to provide a comparison with the British companies. The implication of the figures is that both continental countries have a higher tendency not to sell delivered. (Free frontier, an irrelevant term in British trade from an island, is often used on the European mainland and is taken here to equate to FOB.)

These results emphasize the complexity of the terms of trade issue. Preferred terms can vary from firm to firm and from country to country. In Holland for example freight is reportedly controlled by purchasing management who have a different orientation compared with the British shipping

Table 4
Preferred terms of trade, French and German companies

German %	French %	
30.0	24.0	Ex-works
62.5	48.0	FOB and Free Frontier
7.5	4.0	C and F
5.0	4.0	CIF
7.5	24.0	Free delivered
2.5	4.0	No dominant terms

manager or his French and German commercial equivalents.

The finding that companies appear to want to control freight, rather than want a delivered price to compare locally, does not appear totally logical at first sight. Why should companies wish either to control freight or not?

The British shipping manager is certainly concerned about his professional status. This could well motivate him to want to control the freight on both imports and exports, a position the rest of his firm may not wish to put themselves into. However the pattern on actual terms used, and preferred terms, which those who control freight would like to use, are similar indicating that this is not the case.

Another point is that the managers responsible for freight frequently wanted to reduce their own control over it rather than increase it. Probably there are those to whom shipping is very much a part-time activity and one they would rather be without. Those who wanted to increase control could have been the more full-time shipping manager. This interpretation finds some support in the surveys of French and German firms where one is less likely to find a full-time shipping manager and where control over freight is lower.

One further point worth emphasizing on control is that control not only means being able to profit from any freight purchasing or to avoid being overcharged by allowing the other party to buy the freight, it also means control over the movement of goods, their time of despatch for exports and their time of arrival for imports. A company may well want to buy ex-works so that it controls the time the goods arrive at its premises for use in their manufacturing process or for on-sale. Similarly an exporter may wish to time the despatch of a large piece of machinery for his own convenience in clearing space in a warehouse.

Terms of trade and control of freight

The point was made earlier that companies selling ex-works or FOB may frequently control the purchase of freight as agents of the buyer, selling FOB plus services. Clearly the actual terms companies use in trade do not, in this instance, relate to the definitions contained in Incoterms. While the terms are rarely legally binding any arbitration on a dispute caused by a misunderstanding of who controls what may well favour the party who abided by the definition contained in Incoterms. It is essential that traders are precise in their use of terms of trade to the point where any quotation contains reference to the definition to which the exporter is working.

Routing orders

Irrespective of the actual Terms of Trade or who nominates the forwarder or carrier, in practice control over which forwarder or carrier is used can be influenced by the party not purchasing the freight. Complaints from a customer can affect the repeat purchase of the freight service. Another influence is via a routing order.

If the customer is buying ex-works or FOB it is not only his right but his duty to nominate how the goods are carried after the handover point. Frequently the exporter will arrange this for him using his own local knowledge. Just as often the customer will issue a routing order specifying the company to be used.

Routing orders have come under closer scrutiny in recent times since freight firms have used their existence to sell their services to the consignee irrespective of the terms of trade on the traffic in question. They obtain a signed order instructing the consignor to use their services. The routing order is presented by the freight company to the consignor who may, understandably, be reluctant to change, prompted only by a piece of paper originating from the freight firm itself rather than directly from the customer.

New terms

Changing patterns of trade and modes of transport require new terms to be evolved. The most recent additions to the list in Figure 32 are FRC (free carrier) and CIP (freight or carriage and insurance paid) as alternatives to FOB and CIF. FRC appears as a more useful term than FOB although the latter term is likely to continue in common parlance for some considerable time.

	Cost Units
Ex-works	100.0
Packing	2.0
Transport to docks (including FOB charges)	0.8
Sea freight (including documentation)	4.6
Inland freight (including clearance charges)	2.5
Import duties	5.0
Insurance	0.3
Total cost to importer	115.2
Selling price	150.0
Apparent margin	30.2%

The above calculation is based upon a real example where an exporter had been selling ex-works to one particular market. The agent in that market had negotiated a keen price on the grounds that he had to have a price advantage against local competition able to provide excellent delivery and that he had to absorb large overheads in local storage costs.

Thus the exporter was selling ex-works at a price of 100 units and the agent selling locally at 150 units. This seemed reasonable to the exporter until he performed the above calculation where all the intermediate costs are expressed in terms of the same cost units i.e. packing cost on average 2% of the ex-works price, sea freight 4.6% and so on.

The calculation revealed that the agent's margin on the CIF price to himself was a little over 30%. This excluded warehousing costs, any losses (or profits) due to exchange rate movement but was considerably higher than the 15% the exporter believed the agent was receiving.

Despite the additional work, cost and risk involved, the company decided to rent its own warehousing in the country concerned and sell at a local price to the agent, controlling his margin to the more realistic figure of 15%.

After a while it was clear that the agent's selling price was very low. With the exporter controlling delivery to their own warehousing, delivery reliability was not a problem. With the agent's agreement the selling price was raised, with little or no loss of sales, and to the advantage of both sides.

This example holds many lessons. It is an example of the relative costs involved, albeit for only one product and one market, it shows how the costs build up between ex-works and delivered pricing, but above all it demonstrates the advantages to be gained from controlling, or at least investigating, the distribution pipeline.

Changing to delivered pricing

The insurance issue

Insurance means two different things to the exporter. He can insure the goods against loss and damage and he can insure the contract against default by the buyer. Most countries have a national scheme, designed primarily by governments to promote exports, to cover the second type of risk. The details of such schemes are beyond the scope of this book, as is the detail of what is generally referred to as Marine Insurance, a term used to cover all types of insurance, whatever the means of transport, on international trade. It is however within the scope of this chapter to discuss a number of management issues relating to Marine Insurance.

Most carriers have to cover themselves and their clients for loss and damage. But, almost all such required levels of cover are totally inadequate for the value of the majority of goods. Most freight contracts and the national laws pertaining to the carriage of goods specify these *maximum* levels of cover for which the carrier can be held liable whatever the circumstances.

Traders therefore invariably make separate arrangements for insurance. There is however a growing tendency for developing nations to insist on local insurance on imports and even exports. The trader buying ex-works or selling delivered may well find himself dealing with a variety of types of policy affected by different legal codes.

Most traders use an open cover or blanket cover policy where the insurer does not insist on being told in advance what is being insured. Such agreements are usually made subject to certain conditions including a maximum amount to be covered at any one time or in any one year. A blanket cover implies the insurer does not require a listing of items to be covered under the policy whereas open cover normally requires such a schedule.

Whatever the policy type three factors must be borne in mind.

1 The assured has a duty to his insurer to inform him of anything that might affect the latter's view of the risk he is insuring.
2 Unless allowed for in the policy under a 'held covered' clause, goods which have to be described must be described correctly and precisely.
3 Policies vary in the level of risks covered. For example 'free from particular average' cover and 'all risks' policies offer distinctly different levels of cover.

Few readers will regard themselves as insurance experts. Reference can of course be made to a lawyer for advice but a first step would be, to cover the last point, to assemble a list of typical mishaps and ask the insurers to specify what would be covered in the given circumstances, particularly how much would be paid of the selling price of the goods rather than their domestic value.

The first two points are more difficult to manage. Junior staff will frequently be responsible for despatching individual consignments and it is their judgement as to points 1 and 2 that will matter. It is therefore essential that they realize the significance of both points. In practice few problems occur as the shipping manager will be aware of the circumstances where problems might arise (rumours of civil disturbance; changes in product specification; new markets; and so on).

Finally, reverting to the third point, the problems of dealing with different insurance practice and law around the world can be reduced by referring to the International Chamber of Commerce 'Tables of Practical Equivalents in Marine Insurance'.

Keypoints

1 Offering a delivered price may appear to be good marketing but the buyer may wish to control freight himself and be happier with an ex-works or FOB price.
2 Incoterms or other trade terms standards are not necessarily adhered to in practice. Traders must be careful to allow no room for misunderstanding on the terms to which they wish to commit themselves.
3 Routing orders are both a means of establishing who forwards or carries goods and of marketing freight services through consignee selling.

References and further reading

1   DAVIES, G. J. and GUMBRELL, K. A. 'Selling Delivered' *International Freighting Management*, February, 1981.

Incoterms – published by the International Chamber of Commerce Paris but available through local Chambers of Commerce.
Revised American Foreign Trade Definitions – *see* for example, MURR, A. *Export/Import Traffic Management and Forwarding*, 1941, 6th edition, (Cornell Maritime Press, New York, 1979) p. 335 *et seq*.
SCHMITTHOFF, CLIVE *The Law and Practice of International Trade* (Stevens, London various editions).

12
Management controls in international distribution

Few companies seem to apply formal management controls to their shipping departments. This is both symptomatic of the lack of attention paid to the function by senior management and the problems of setting meaningful controls on the function.

Budgetary control

Budgeting is one method of management control which every firm seems to employ. It assists in short-term planning because budgets have to be defined in advance and it assists in control because people have to work within their budget and tend to monitor their expenditure against budget. Budgeting helps companies plan for seasonal fluctuations in expenditure. It helps identify areas for greater examination. But budgeting can be a problem area for freight.

Freight budgets are set, in practice, in one of two main ways, historical trend or a fixed percentage on export value. Both methods are suspect for freight because of the way expenditure can vary as the terms of delivery vary. For example, a change in terms from FOB to CIF means greater expenditure on freight by the company while they are selling the same quantity. A company selling on FOB plus services terms could change to freight forward and not pay the freight themselves, making it appear that freight expenditure has fallen. A freight budget can be underspent or overspent because of changes in terms of trade or because the trade pattern itself changes between markets which demand different terms of trade.

Budgeting for freight on terms of a percentage of export value can be attractive because of its simplicity. Export sales have to be estimated anyway for the coming year so why not use this budget figure to derive a freight budget? (Occasionally this is done without the shipping manager's knowledge leaving him to work to a budget he had no part in setting!) As before, a change in the markets served or in the mix of products or in the method of freighting can make a nonsense of the budget.

Using the percentage method of estimating freight within a firm can cause problems outside budgeting. One engineering company used a figure of 7% to estimate costs. This was a fair average to take over all markets and all products. Unfortunately the practice was extended to quotations for potential business. Buyers were sent quotations for machinery on an FOB basis with a 7% mark-up for CIF. The clients who would have paid more for freight gladly accepted the CIF price. Those who would have paid less but who wanted a delivered price were annoyed by what appeared to be overcharging. The process of quotation is extended if the shipping manager has to become involved to provide a freight cost but it is sometimes well worthwhile.

Other problems with estimating freight using a percentage of export value

---

It is vital for the shipping manager to become involved in setting any freight budget. After all he is likely to be appraised as a buyer against any budget figures.

It is equally important that he is able to estimate a realistic figure rather than pull one out of thin air. He must be able therefore to estimate the pattern of next year's exports and the trends of freight costs. The first he has no control over and no responsibility for, but export sales will have their own estimates formal or informal. As to trends in freight costs, good records are the key together with the kind of information often contained in predictive articles in the trade press.

A computerized export system should hold freight costs, by

product, mode and market if possible. A manual filing system invariably has this data available.

Productivity

Productivity has been the most prominent business term in the 1980s. The word is much abused. It is taken to mean output per man rather than cost per output. In distribution, with the problems of using freight expenditure budgets as identified above, the emphasis has been on the volume of export business handled per employee.

As is the problem with all such ratios, an improvement in the ratio itself can be made by increasing the volume of business or decreasing the number of staff. Either makes the ratio look as if it is showing an improvement but there is a limit on how much work any person can handle before they become inefficient and the real cost of their output rises rather than falls.

Another problem with ratios is knowing whether one company's output per man is good or bad in absolute terms. If comparable data can be obtained from other companies this can provide some indication of relative performance. How valid this is depends on the measures used.

Companies rarely serve the same markets with the same products in the same quantities. Export value per employee is then not a good ratio to apply. It may take less work to arrange the export of ten container loads of goods from America to Canada than to send one air freight to Mexico.

Another snag is the part-time nature in many firms of export distribution and the way the function is sometimes closely integrated with other areas such as export sales. It is not always possible to be precise on how much of one person's time is spent on the area.

However none of the very real problems noted here make it either impossible or undesirable to calculate at least one productivity ratio: the number of export consignments handled per employee in the shipping department. The use of the consignment as a base is better for comparison than tonnage, value or units of production, (although some firms may find it difficult to differentiate between an order for many different products which are despatched simultaneously and a large single order).

Table 5 contains the results of one study of 139 exporters in Britain, France, and Germany.[1] There is a relationship between department size and the number of consignments handled although it is by no means precise. It was sometimes difficult to do more than estimate the data in Table 5. Nevertheless the table does allow a quick absolute measure. The further to the top right-hand corner of the table a company finds itself the more it needs to ask itself about its efficiency and cost of handling work. If the firm finds itself well over towards the bottom left of the table it may mean that too much is being demanded of individuals or that most of the work is being done by outsiders, the freight forwarders.

Table 5
Number of employees handling consignment numbers.
Sources: *Gumbrell, K. A. PhD thesis Manchester Polytechnic, 1983 Graph SITPRO.*

Consignments handled per annum	Size of Department (number of employees)				
	1	2–4	5–10	11–20	21+
<100	8	4	2		
100 – 499	11	13	3	2	
500 – 999		8	5	1	
1,000 – 4,999	6	22	19	5	3
5,000 – 9,999		1	3	5	2
10,000 +		1	6	4	5

In a study of 30 British companies[2] by SITPRO the number of consignments per employee was found to range from 100 to 750 with a mean of 330. When this average is sketched on to Table 5 it demonstrates how wide is the spread of apparent relative efficiency.

In the SITPRO study values were obtained for the complete cost per consignment. The authors quote an American study indicating costs averaging $7\frac{1}{2}\%$ of consignment value accounted for by export procedures (excluding freight) and state that their findings indicate a similar percentage in Britain.

Their detailed analysis of administration costs included data on salaries, form costs, operational costs, establishment costs and freight forwarder's costs. Of these, salaries, establishment costs and forwarder's costs were the most significant in ascending order.

They also tried to estimate cost penalties such as the cost of errors or delays. The range of estimates for the percentage of consignments delayed ranged from below 1% to over 30%. However many problems were claimed to be outside of the control of the exporter. This introduces another possible management control criterion, error rate. A shipping clerk's accuracy on typing in information to a computerized export system can be monitored, although the value of doing so is questionable.

One firm, ICI Pharmaceuticals, used a voluntary method of error recording. Staff were asked to record any error they made which may have affected the customer. For the idea to work, the subordinate has to be confident that what is happening is not meant primarily to assess him or her as an individual. The main objective is to identify areas for improvement in the clerical systems and knowledge level of the staff. Any problems with the latter can help define training needs.

A feature of personal assessment in many sales forces is an annual test of product knowledge. The idea can be transferred to shipping. If an exporter is looking to replace the forwarding role with its own staff they must be equally knowledgeable about the nuances of documentation and the relevant parts of the freight and forwarding industry. Formal qualifications or performance in an annual quiz are two measures of staff which should not be ignored as they can relate directly to efficiency.

Credit control

One area which is sometimes included in the span of control of the shipping manager is credit control. Many managers who have this responsibility do not relish it. It is after all a specialist area involving decisions on whether to extend credit, how much and how long, and how hard to push for payment.

The shipping manager may feel that he is better left out of any discussions or arguments over credit. He has to form a good working relationship with the customer. On the other hand he has, next to sales, the best knowledge of the customer.

Most countries have some form of cheap credit or credit insurance available for the exporter sponsored by national government. The way the systems work varies but essentially the credit risk is limited in its total value for each country and for each importer. Large orders do have to be cleared in advance with the credit agency to ensure that individual or national limits are not exceeded.

Many firms deal on open account with exports. This is logical when trading with a subsidiary or a long-standing customer in a developed and stable economy. A problem can be the great difference in credit expected by various nationalities. With some countries what looks like extended credit is normal practice, in others, extensions to credit are deliberate delaying tactics by the buyer. Fortunately guides are available indicating the length and nature of normal credit terms expected allowing the exporter to set his pricing policy and run the credit control to obtain his money without upsetting the client.[3]

Even if the shipping manager is not responsible for credit control, if he is responsible for order processing, he will need to maintain a close liaison with whoever does deal with credit control. Once an order has been acknowledged it can damage an exporter's reputation to have to write to the potential importer declining his offer.

A client survey

Managing a department depends on individual skill and also on knowledge. Firms seem willing to accept ideas on gathering information on what is happening inside their firm but are curiously reluctant to ask their customers what they think of them.

Perhaps firms are concerned about giving customers an opportunity for frivolous complaint. But the act of sending a brief questionnaire on the level of service they receive is in itself of value in convincing the customer that he is dealing with a firm and a shipping department who are concerned to give him the best possible service. It is better to know about any problems immediately rather than find out after the customer has taken his business elsewhere or has written to complain.

The quality of service offered by a forwarder or carrier is difficult to measure. A customer's opinion can be useful in confirming a good impression or in negotiating better service when reviewing an existing contract.

Some firms do send short questionnaires every year to their customers enquiring about levels of service, damage to goods, local delivery costs and other factors pertaining to the interchange of goods and money. Every firm should follow this example.

The value of the order pipeline

The main emphasis of this book is on evolving a more systematic approach to international physical distribution so that a firm can claim with some justification to be running an export and/or an import logistics operation rather than the *ad hoc* approach so commonly found in practice.

Management theories, such as logistics, cannot provide an instant answer to practical problems. Each firm is a special case. But theory can guide the practitioner to rethink a situation which has become too familiar and difficult to see objectively. The logistics concept is a valid method of doing this. However the value of any change in approach has to be assessable and assessable in financial terms.

Total Distribution Cost analysis is one analytical tool to assess the value of changing the physical distribution system but it cannot assess the value of changing the management system. Neither can it be used to control that system.

SITPRO's costing guidelines and the equivalent techniques referred to as the Distribution Audit[4] offer a checklist approach to calculating the true costs of distribution and its management. If such studies are conducted regularly then they constitute a form of control but one which is complex to institute.

Other methods of control such as budget costs and productivity measures all have their problems of precision.

There is one method of assessment that can be used for control, which gets to the real heart of the internal objectives of any management system and which includes one measure of customer service. This is the value of the outstanding order pipeline.

From the moment the order arrives it is in the firm's interest to get the order processed, despatched and paid for as quickly as possible. It is also in the customer's interest to be given the best possible delivery time (unless his order is for a particular delivery schedule).

This view of export logistics is more valid for the high repeat order company. The firm producing custom-built products will have similar pressures but these will be on the design team and manufacturing. Once the goods are ready for despatch, however, the same pressures apply to shipping. Finished goods cost money to keep within the firm, the opportunity cost of their value in materials and wages, the opportunity cost of the revenue to the firm, let alone the costs of storage. Orders unmet mean revenue and profit unreceived and customers unsatisfied who may well take their custom elsewhere.

A E Auto Parts, a British exporter of automotive components, has applied the value of the outstanding order pipeline as a key measure of its shipping function for many years. The value to them is a single figure, easily understood both in the shipping department and elsewhere in the firm, which provides a valid measure of what is happening in the shipping element in export.

Two problems can occur when using the idea. Shipping may be unwilling to accept a provisional order into their pipeline. If the order has no letter of credit, or the credit worthiness of the customer has not been defined, the order may reside in the system, perhaps with stock allocated to it, for some time with little the shipping function can do to convert it to a dispatchable order.

Secondly the concept encourages the dispatch of part orders rather than waiting for a full order to be completed. This means proportionally higher freight bills. Similarly consolidation of orders into more economic units is effectively discouraged. Nevertheless the concept is the only one known to the author that has been proven in practice.

With the availability of quantifiable management controls emanating from a computerized export system and applied to a systems based shipping function the title of export logistics department is credible. Some companies are well placed to use this approach in its entirety. All will benefit from using some, if not all, of the ideas that are contained in the previous chapters.

Keypoints

1 Formal management controls are not always applied to international distribution.
2 Budgetary control and productivity measured by consignments handled per employee are two controls which should be considered.
3 Shippers should conduct a client survey.
4 The value of the order pipeline is recommended as a key control.

References and further reading

1 GUMBRELL, K. A. PhD thesis (Manchester Polytechnic, 1983).
2 SITPRO Costing Guidelines for Export Administration (SITPRO, London, 1979).
3 HEWSON, T. L. Notes on Western Europe. Private publication for the Institute of Credit Management.

4 BREAM, ROLAND and WILSON SMITH, JOHN *Distribution Audit Workbook* (Centre for Physical Distribution Management, London, 1978).

PART THREE
The international distribution industry

Moving goods from seller to buyer is big business. Over the years the average number of miles goods travel during the process has increased. Spiralling oil prices may have checked this trend as companies rethink their distribution strategies but the constant demand for 'something different' from the consumer would indicate that, unless and until oil prices begin to surge ahead once more, goods will be moved ever further to be sold.

These statements are true of both domestic and international markets. Goods moving internationally will sooner or later join a domestic system. The following chapters concentrate on the transport modes and the organizations more likely to be associated with such modes. The larger the domestic market the harder it is to differentiate between the two industries. However the international side is typified by the strong presence of a middle man, the international freight forwarder, who traditionally owns no transport (other than collect and delivery vehicles); the long distances in transit; the problems of moving goods between different countries with different legal systems including the complicating factor of customs.

The international distribution industry is one of the largest and most long-standing industries in the world. Shipping is a significant source of foreign exchange earnings for many countries. While it may be a traditional industry it has been constantly evolving since the early days of domination by sailing ships and canal barges. Air freight was unknown fifty years ago, and containerization of liner trades dates from the mid 1950s. Roll-on roll-off ferries were pioneered by converted tank landing ships left over from the Second World War while the type of vessel which is a common sight throughout the world, the RoRo ship, arrived as late as the 1960s. The container revolution has tended to overshadow the development of specialist vessels and the fact that conventional shipping still has a significant role to play.

Technical change has initiated change in the way shipping companies are organized. Across the North Atlantic for example, while the tonnage carried has increased, the number of vessels carrying the trade has declined. Separate lines have given way to consortia each member selling space on the same vessel.

The final part of this book aims to describe many of the more significant points about the industry which forms a vital part of the international logistics system.

13
The freight forwarder

This is adapted from 'International Freight Forwarding: a comparison between the United Kingdom and the United States', a paper presented at the AIB Conference in Barcelona, December 1981, by the author and Dr Gary N. Dicer of the University of Tennessee.

The origins of today's middle man in the international physical distribution industry can be traced back to well before modern trading patterns became established. Murr links him to the 'Frachter' who, in the 1300s in Europe, combined forwarding and carriage with the physical protection of the merchant and his goods.[1] By the end of the eighteenth century the expeditor of freight movements was referred to as a 'spediteur', a term which persists today. Another publication traces the origin of at least part of the London forwarding community to certain publicans in the City of London being asked to 'hold and reforward' the goods of merchants founding their fortunes in the Americas.[2] Soon, we are told, the business of international freight forwarding outgrew even the hotel business. A third source goes back even further, to the tenth century, where the author identifies the emergence of a 'third party whose characteristics were that he owned neither goods nor means of transport'.[3] The idea of a forwarder as a middle man in freight persists to this day but has become, in recent times, substantially modified.

If the origins of the forwarder cannot be traced precisely then neither can the role of the latter-day forwarder be defined with any precision. A publication by NEDO entitled 'The Freight Forwarder' points out that 'it is not easy to define with any precision what and who is a freight forwarder or indeed what is forwarding.'[4] The constitution of the British Institute of Freight Forwarders begs the question with the definition 'Forwarder means any person engaged in the business of forwarding as generally understood', while the US Federal Maritime Commission regards forwarding as 'the preparation and processing of international transport documents, the co-ordination of transport, including the provision of warehousing and the giving of expert advice'.

Despite the problems of definition all sources are agreed that forwarding is an important function in international trade. The way the forwarding industry is organized and the way it develops is then of concern to the shipping manager. This chapter aims to compare the forwarding function in Britain and the USA. The choice of these two countries is significant in that the USA is seeking to expand its relatively low contribution to national income from export and the UK is evolving from the world-wide trading nation, which is highly dependent on trade for its livelihood, to part of a European Community where trading patterns can be expected to evolve towards a pattern more like those of domestic trading between the various states of the Union.

In addition, both countries have approached forwarding, from a governmental policy perspective, in opposite directions. Under the British system, forwarding is unregulated and subject mainly to commercial competitive pressures or industry self-regulation. While, in the United States, the freight forwarder is under the jurisdiction of the Federal Maritime Commission, which controls much of its activity. Oddly, both countries have been considering adopting the other's policy towards this industry.

The role of the freight forwarder

Trade estimates for the proportion of traffic handled by freight forwarders vary but a reasonable consensus would be that between 80% and 95% of airfreight and about 50% of surface freight is purchased through, or controlled by, freight forwarders.

One of the problems of any more precise measure, apart from the lack of published data, is that of definition. The traditional freight forwarder, a middle man who is unassociated with the ownership of transport and is solely the agent of the trader, is no longer dominant. While few forwarders are associated by ownership with shipping lines and especially airlines, many are associated, directly or by common ownership, with domestic and international road transport. The traditional ship's agent, or broker, who sold space for a shipping line, now often acts also as a general forwarder. The titles 'agent' and 'shipping agent' were dropped from the British professional institute in 1970 when the title 'Institute of Freight Forwarders' was adopted.

Size and structure

In Great Britain, *The Institute of Freight Forwarders (IFF) Year Book* for 1980/81 listed 753 trading members. Of these 488 were parent companies and 265 associated with one of these parents. The Institute estimates that there are 'probably over one thousand companies operating as freight forwarders in the UK'[5] A survey commissioned by the International Freight Forwarding Training Council (IFFTC) between May and August 1979 obtained three estimates of the number of freight forwarders.[6] Their best estimate was 3,270 freight forwarding units (including branches and sole traders) and 2,725 freight forwarding companies. A study attributed to FIATA, the international association of national forwarding bodies, puts the number of forwarding enterprises as 1,500.[7] The IFFTC survey estimated that 56,270 people were employed in forwarding.

The various estimates of size of the forwarding industry are not then compatible. The numerical differences cannot however be explained by differences of definition as even the Institute's membership lists contain forwarder-operators as well as the traditional forwarding firm with no links to any transport concern.

Table 6
Structure of the UK Forwarding Industry:
Percentage of firms by size (measured by numbers of employees)

	1–15	16–50	51–100	101–200	201+
% of Firms	55	28	9	5	3

Source: [7] From a study by FIATA

One explanation for the discrepancy is the large number of very small companies who trade as forwarders (*see* Table 6), very often sole traders, who survive by offering expertise to a limited number of usually small, local companies. There is, in the UK, little or no control over an individual or a company offering itself for business as a freight forwarder. The issue of regulation is discussed later but one of the consequences of the lack of formal regulation is the existence of many small firms. Perhaps as a further consequence freight forwarding concerns come and go, often quite frequently.

In a project conducted by Charmaine Gunton of Manchester Polytechnic (Table 7) a list was made of all companies in the area of the Greater Manchester Council (population 2.697 million, area 495 sq miles) who offered international freight and forwarding services.[8] The initial list of 312 compiled from current directories and the like was used as a mailing list. Some 80 letters were returned by the Post Office as 'gone away'. The firm concerned had either ceased trading, closed a regional office, been taken over, or, in a minority of cases, moved out of the area. Most fell into the first two categories.

The Greater Manchester Council area is not unrepresentative of the UK, as a whole, in that it has its own port and airport and it is well served by international road and rail freight terminals. Further evidence on the structure of the forwarding industry is available in two financial analyses of forwarding companies.[9] Baxter and Allera conclude from reviewing one of the studies,[10] that the industry is one where there are a large number of companies operating at low levels of activity, and a relatively small number of large organiza-

Table 7

Survey of Forwarders and Forwarder Operators in Greater Manchester 1980–1

Original mailing list of companies offering international services	312
Companies who had 'gone away'	80
Companies who were still trading, but who had ceased to offer an international service	9
Companies taken over by others	4
Companies apparently offering international services	219
Primarily domestic transport companies known to offer international forwarding services	20
Total known forwarder and forwarder operators	239
Of these, 108 responded to a questionnaire survey	108
Primary role of respondents (including multiple replies)	
Shipping lines	13
Road haulers	42
Airline	10
Loading broker/shipping agent	15
Freight forwarder	74
	154
Of the 74, whose primary role(s) included freight forwarder, 42 nominated only that role	
Members of the IFF listed under Greater Manchester 1980–1	92

NOTE: A company with more than one office is only counted once.

tions. The profit levels recorded by both financial surveys show that forwarding is not, at least on paper, a highly profitable business in the UK. ICC describes the profit figures recorded in their survey as 'totally inadequate' and both surveys record numerous loss-making concerns. This view of the industry needs to be seen in the context of a growth in tonnage in British trade (with a slight hiccup for the oil crisis) until the world-wide recession and the monetarist policies of the UK Government started to be felt in 1980–1.

Within the overall pattern of few companies of any size and few which are highly profitable it is interesting to look more closely at some exceptions. The Lep group Ltd, consistently heads any UK table based on turnover and their record shows a relatively consistent history of profit. The Group's 1979 turnover was £62 million from 2,402 employees and their pretax profits at £6.77 million appear large against those of their competition.[11] The Lep group is, perhaps significantly, a highly diversified and international company. Most of its activities are directly related to international transport, forwarding, international road haulage, airfreight forwarding chartering, packing and specialized bloodstock forwarding. However, the group does have interests in travel, general insurance and pensions funding. Nevertheless the company's main business is associated with international distribution which provides them with a satisfactory 17.5% return on net assets employed.

Air Shipping Agencies Ltd*, was another exception to the stereotype poor profit level and has held the claim to be Britain's most profitable company. Their 1978 turnover was £3.35 million from 215 employees providing profits of £0.55 million.

Three of the top twenty private companies in 1979 were involved in international distribution when assessed by the ratio of pretax profit over net tangible assets.[12] This underlines the alternative view of forwarding as a potentially profitable business requiring limited capital investment with the possibility therefore of relatively large returns on investment.

The structure of the industry in the United States is somewhat different from that of Great Britain, both in size and number of firms, as well as their legal form. There are four major categories of international intermediary – the Foreign Freight Forwarder, the Customs House Broker, the Non-Vessel Operating Common Carrier, and the Air Freight Forwarder. All four institutions fall under some type of governmental regulation. While they are identified as separate

*Since renamed.

entities for regulatory purposes, common ownership is possible. For example, it is quite common to find a single firm serving as both a foreign freight forwarder and a customs house broker.

Unlike the British system with freedom of entry and exit from the industry, forwarding in the United States is tightly controlled. Licences or permits are required from the appropriate administrative body before business can be transacted. Turnover in the industry remains small as the regulatory agencies attempt to limit entry to only a sufficient number of firms who can effectively provide service at a viable profit level. Although there are small-size firms, the tendency is for medium-to large-scale operations with offices in various locations to give broad geographical coverage.

In terms of numbers, there are approximately 600 corporate firms licensed as customs house brokers, 35 licensed partnerships and over 2,000 licensed individuals. There are 1,000 firms licensed as foreign freight forwarders.

The special case of the air forwarder

There is a limited amount of specialization and segmentation of the freight market by forwarders. Some specialize by product, e.g. shoes, computers, hanging garments, bloodstock, household removals, hazardous goods, oversize loads, exhibition equipment. Often this specialization is on the basis of offering special equipment. Frequently any specialization is an offshoot of a larger forwarding concern rather than the *raison d'être* for a single company. Other companies specialize by consignment size, e.g. bulk, full loads, groupage or express groupage.

In Great Britain, many, often smaller companies, specialize by market. This, in part, reflects the size distribution in the industry with a large number of forwarder/operators serving different parts of the European market (which now accounts for over 50% of UK trade) and the way a small company evolves in the industry. Many firms form agreements with other similar companies in countries to which they wish to consign. The agreements are to find freight for each other especially to fill the backload for an outgoing lorry. A British forwarder/operator will then refer to the quality of his agents in France and Germany when selling his services. The example cited earlier of Lep as a truly international company is not typical of the industry whose members rely on their correspondents abroad to provide them with their international presence.

The dominant criterion for specialization in the UK and USA forwarding industry is transport mode and specifically that between surface and airfreight. The airfreight forwarder, although he might be linked to a general forwarder or transport operator, is himself solely concerned with airfreight. The larger British agencies are licensed by IATA (the International Air Transport Association) who represent the interests of member airlines. Non-IATA airforwarders do exist but rely upon sub-agency agreements with the IATA agents.

The structure of the airfreight agency sector can be gathered from the apparently private, but frequently published, IATA Revenue Returns. Forwarders' incomes will be somewhat larger than these returns because of charges to shippers and revenue from non-IATA airlines. They do provide a similar picture to that for all forwarders of a large number of relatively small companies in Great Britain, and fewer medium- to large-size firms in the United States.

The UK had 157 IATA agents in 1980 of which 50 lodged returns exceeding £1 million.[13] Only 5 exceeded £10 million with the market leader Pandair at £17 million. Total IATA billings in the UK for 1980 were £221 million with the top 20% of companies billing nearly 80% of the total. There are, it is estimated, 350 specialist air forwarders in the UK with nearly half neither licensed by IATA nor members of the Institute of Freight Forwarders.[14]

IATA has a formal application system where the applicant has to provide evidence on facilities and quality of staff for example. A panel of airline representatives then vet each application. IATA reserves the right to terminate agency agreements or to fine agents in breach of IATA rules.

The UK and US air forwarder differs from his surface

counterpart in a number of ways. He is, because of the nature of his industry, well placed to offer a service which is truly international. Many exporters will employ a very limited number of airfreight agents and are more likely to use an agent in buying airfreight.

In an unpublished British telephone survey of 200 exporters randomly selected from the circulation list of a trade publication, 17 had no airfreight agent (because they had no cause to use airfreight), 165 always bought airfreight through an agent while only 74 always bought surface freight through an agent. 95 of the airfreight users were asked for the number of airfreight agents they used, 62(65%) used only 1 agent, unless the consignment was routed by the customer. The minority that used more than one agent of their own nomination were equally divided in their reason for doing so between requiring competition and because of the (geographical) specialization of the agent.

This picture must be compared with the results of another survey of the use of forwarders where 80% of companies used up to 10 different forwarders in total.[15] While it is believed that the last statistics should be interpreted to mean forwarder and forwarder/operator, they do confirm the practical difference in usage of the two types of forwarder, air and surface, with the latter's, often geographical, specialization.

Regulation

As has been previously mentioned, the most visible difference between the US and the UK is in the area of government regulation of forwarders and other intermediaries. The traditional attitudes toward the industry may seem incongruous with their political policies on economic matters.

The British, who have been much more active in government involvement and control of business in general, and transport in particular, have left the forwarding function alone. The United States, on the other hand, with a long history of limited government controls on business, has developed a substantial regulatory mechanism for international forwarding operations.

There is no formal regulation of the UK freight forwarder by licensing and, with the exception of the IATA agency, there is little to stop any one person or company from offering services to the exporter and transport company. There is no regulation on who is able to make out customs entries. In 1970 a NEDO committee examining the role of the forwarder concluded that 'insufficient justification exists for any form of statutory regulation of the industry'. Individuals from both sides of the industry are often quoted in the trade press voicing contrary opinions. Forwarders are concerned with standards but will also be conscious of the erosion, by shippers themselves, of the forwarder's traditional sources of revenue in preparing documentation and purchasing freight.

The Institute of Freight Forwarders in Britain has the dual role of professional institute and trade association. In its first role it sets examinations to establish standards of professional qualification and exercises disciplinary supervision to safeguard the professional standing of its members. In its second role it negotiates with other bodies involved with international distribution, including carriers, ports and government and it issues standard trading conditions which most members use in their dealings with shippers. The two areas of disciplinary supervision and trading condition are those most relevant to the issue of regulation.

As for discipline the IFF cannot impose its authority on non-members. Tudhope from the IFF implied in an article on the forwarder that non-membership does have a restrictive effect on a forwarder's ability to trade, as for example the IFF is the only source of the FIATA FBL.[16] The FBL is a negotiable document of title that can be used to cover combined transport operations. Alternatives exist but advantages are claimed for the FIATA document.

An investigation which began in 1974 under the 1948 Companies Act against the UK arm of Kuehne and Nagel culminated in that company's being expelled from the IFF. The investigation in 1974 was concerned with the certain malpractices.[17] After expulsion the company continued to trade both in the UK and around the world. They are a large company, at the time of the enquiry with 7,000 staff world-wide, but they are not based in the UK. How much the publicity has affected their business or how much expulsion meant to them and the clients they retained has to be left as opinion. However, from 1975 to 1977 turnover remained level at £22 million and profits went from £59,000 to £1,000 with a £49,000 loss in 1976. The number of UK employees decreased from 498 to 392. But by 1979 the company was referring to a projected annual turnover of £34 million for a new UK holding company that would be their second largest in Europe (the company had its head office in Switzerland).

As for trading conditions, the IFF was challenged in 1981 by the Freight Transport Association (FTA). The FTA found the IFF's 1980–1 conditions 'unacceptable'.[18] The FTA and its constituent part, the British Shipper's Council, represents the transportation and distribution interests of British trade and industry. The FTA complained to the Office of Fair Trading and asked for the conditions to be put before the Restrictive Practices Court. The core of the objection was about the liability of the forwarder to the shipper. The IFF conditions specify proof of 'wilful neglect' as the criterion for compensation.

Schmithoff's standard legal text on international trade and transport acknowledges the special agency role of the forwarder and that the IFF's Trading Conditions do modify the general law on agencies.[19] In the specific case of liability a general agent would have to exercise 'diligence and whatever skill is professed', rather than, as the IFF's conditions would prefer avoid 'willful neglect'.

The issue of the legal status of the forwarder is relevant to the issue of regulation. The traditional forwarder can be regarded at least, in part, as the shipper's legal agent. The modern forwarder is often a carrier and therefore also a principal. The FTA objected to what they saw as the different way the IFF's conditions treated the forwarder acting in either role. It is tempting to suggest that formal regulation may be necessary to clarify such confusion unless both parties agree to a form of trading conditions.

To demonstrate whether the IFF can then be regarded as an effective alternative to formal regulation is not then possible.

Expulsion does not deny the ability to trade on a significant, and relatively extensive, scale and the IFF has been in dispute with the representatives of its customers on its trading conditions.

Regulation, would, however, be unlikely to be effective without restriction, which could include the restriction of shippers to conduct their own forwarding and dealing with customs.

In the United States, the different forms of intermediary are regulated by various governmental agencies. In the case of firms which offer multiple services this often results in jurisdictional overlap between regulatory bodies. When issues of large national interests arise this can lead to inter-agency disputes as to regulatory authority, with the firm caught in the middle. An example was the disagreement over the appropriate agency to control 'mini land bridge' service and rates.

The major regulatory body over international trade in the US is the Federal Maritime Commission. The Commission was established in August 1961 under a Presidential reorganization plan. However, some form of government regulation dates back as early as the Shipping Act of 1916 and grows continually stronger over the years. The Commission has responsibility for regulation of common carriers by water in international trade, terminal operators in connection with oceangoing carriers, and independent ocean freight forwarders.

The role of the Commission in regulation of foreign freight forwarders is primarily aimed at preventing discriminatory practices against shippers, and they extend Commission control over the carriers. Since the forwarder is an active intermediary between shipper and carrier, the Congress felt it necessary to bring this function under regulation if the intent of Congress was to be effectively carried out. The law primarily controls the industry through a licensing process. Thus, any person carrying on the business of forwarding, where they have no beneficial interest in the shipment, is required to obtain a licence from the Commission. Licensing is not automatic, and the applicant must prove that he is qualified, fit, willing and able to perform the functions of forwarding. The Commission also has the authority to revoke a licence for failure to comply with Commission orders, rules, and regulations.

Thus the foreign freight forwarder finds himself regulated, primarily to prevent discriminatory practices between shipper and carrier. Under US law, the foreign freight forwarder is clearly acting as an agent for the shipper and assumes no rights or responsibilities as a common carrier. This is a sharp distinction from the common carrier status of US domestic freight forwarders. Also, unlike the US, the British make no such distinction between foreign and domestic forwarders, although the size of the latter country means only limited potential for a true forwarder rather than a carrier. Domestic forwarding in US is regulated by a separate agency, the Interstate Commerce Commission.

Complicating the situation, as to legal status and licensing, has been the recent rise of intermodalism and containerization with the attendant development of a new form of intermediary. This consolidator of intermodal and international freight, the Non-Vessel Operating Common Carrier, is a departure from the traditional role of a simple agent played by the forwarder. This resulted in a jurisdictional dispute between the Interstate Commerce Commission and the Federal Maritime Commission. In 1982, at least, the NVOCC was treated as a common carrier with responsibility for filing and publishing tariffs, similar to an ocean carrier.

A second major controlling agency is the US Treasury, Customs Service. All persons who desire to act as agents for importers in their customs transactions are required, by law, to be licensed by the US Customs Service. The licence is only issued based on the individual's knowledge of customs regulations and their general character. A stringent examination is required as well as a personal background investigation. Licences can be issued to a corporation if at least two of the principal officers hold a broker's licence. These licences may be revoked for malpractice by the Secretary of the Treasury.

Finally the international air freight forwarder in the US is regulated not only by the IATA requirements mentioned previously in the British case, but by the Civil Aeronautics

Board (CAB). They are considered an 'indirect' carrier. This means that they issue their own way bills and then act as shipper in their relationship with the air carrier. The airfreight forwarder is only responsible for registering with the CAB and is not required to show need or obtain a certificate of convenience and necessity. Under the airline deregulation legislation passed in the US, even this limited form of control has been eliminated.

The erosion of the forwarder's role

The move by shippers towards replacing the traditional forwarding function with a partial in-house function has been identified earlier when it was argued that this could contribute to greater effectiveness in exporting.

In a survey in 1977, both forwarders and shippers tended to agree to the proposition that there was a trend for the exporter to move into the forwarder's area of documentation and transportation but at the same time many shippers felt that the forwarder's role would expand in importance to a manufacturing company.[20] The two opinions can only be compatible if the forwarder becomes a forwarder/operator or offers other services to replace those being undertaken in-house.

A reasonable generalization on the British freight industry would be that as the British forwarder has found his traditional source of income eroded by a number of factors he has moved more into other areas and particularly into European transportation. This move has been paralleled by a number of domestic road hauliers becoming European forwarder-operators.

It would be logical to expect that as the European Economic Community evolves into a truly domestic market, with a reduction in trade formalities, or even their complete elimination, the concept of a 'domestic' transport company serving one national area will become at least partially redundant. Currently comparatively few transport concerns involve themselves both nationally and internationally and, when they do so, not under the same limited company. This pattern repeats itself across Europe.

Of an estimated 5,000 West German transport firms only 1,000 are involved internationally. Corresponding estimates for France are 2,850 and 800.[7] In the Manchester survey referred to earlier, of 822 domestic road hauliers in the Greater Manchester Council area surveyed, only 20 offered international forwarding services and 17 moved goods internationally (presumably as subcontractors for forwarders) but did not offer any forwarding service.

The lack of integration between domestic and international road transportation in Europe is partly a function of the structure of the industry which is dominated by the smaller company who might not have the resources to offer even a complete coverage of the domestic market. However, from the viewpoint of the transport user he has to approach a number of different organizations to expedite the movement of his goods within, what should become, a homogenous market. The complexity of the UK international freight market can be judged from the results of the Manchester study; a shipper is faced with carrier choice, mode choice and whether to deal through a traditional forwarder.

Future trends

Two issues have to be faced in the UK, regulation and the consequences of a domestic market on the scale of the EEC. Calls for regulation have come from both shippers and forwarders but both stand to lose if regulatory systems similar to those in other countries are adopted. The shipper could lose his flexibility to undertake his own forwarding and customs' dealings while the forwarder will have to deal with the bureaucracy of any formal system of control. Both sides would benefit, the shipper in feeling greater confidence in his dealings with the forwarder and the forwarder in the exclusion of both shippers and perhaps carriers from his area of work. The larger forwarder could welcome the opportunity to limit the scope for the smaller firm.

The carriers may have mixed feelings on the issue. Airlines have been markedly reluctant to involve themselves in freight or in dealing with other than the very largest of shippers and have evolved a licensing system through IATA which acts as a regulatory system, but one which they themselves control. Shipping lines and road hauliers may see regulation as limiting their ability to deal directly with the shipper.

Many EEC countries have some form of regulation and such is the nature of decision making in the Community that established regulatory systems tend to be adopted across the Community. If this is the case in freight, the international/EEC forwarder may well become more like his transatlantic counterpart, involved both domestically and internationally, and subject to greater and more formal regulation.

In contrast to the British trend, the US approach will most likely be to eliminate or greatly reduce the amount of regulation now in effect. This has already been seen in the case of international air shipments. As both political parties seem to be in agreement on the de-regulation of the transportation industry in general, and for the 'market place' to act as the controller of rates and service, it can be expected that this philosophy will spill over to the international shipments moving by sea. Although it is probable that complete elimination of regulation on the international intermediary will not come about, it is likely that some relaxation of un-needed or burdensome requirements will.

It is an interesting conjecture to foresee that, by the end of the decade, the United States will have adopted the current British policy towards forwarding, and the UK will have adopted the US stand. However, the more likely results will be a continuous movement on the part of both countries away from their current policy dichotomies toward a more homogenous approach to this important member of an international transaction.

Keypoints

1 The forwarder, traditionally the middle man of the freight industry, is now not so easy to define. Forwarders are frequently significant carriers in their own right.
2 The forwarder's legal status is difficult to define. He

cannot be regarded uniquely as the agent of the exporter or importer.

3 The forwarder is only partially regulated in Britain but almost totally regulated in the USA. It is possible that both systems will move somewhat closer over the years.

4 The trader must be confident that the forwarder, whether regulated or not, is going to represent his interests competently and that his financial status is reliable. Licensing or professional examination or membership of a professional institute is at least a partial answer to the first issue.

References and further reading

1 MURR, A. Export/Import Traffic Management and Forwarding, sixth ed. (Cornell Maritime Press, New York, 1979), p. 1.

2 ANON. *Understanding the Freight Business*, 2nd edn, Thomas Meadows Co. Ltd, London, 1970, p. 13.

3 ANTAL, G. 'The Scientific Basis of Freight Forwarding' Lloyds List 18.12.80. p. 6.

4 NEDO, 'The Freight Forwarder' (HMSO, London, 1970), p. 1.

5 GATES, A. C. 'A Brief Introduction to Freight Forwarding' Institute of Freight Forwarders Ltd, p. 13, undated.

6 HOWARD, P. L. *et al.* 'Survey of Manpower and Training Needs of the Freight Forwarding Industry', IFFTC 1980.

7 FFCAT 'Transport et Distribution Internationale des Merchandises', Federation Francaise des Commissionaires et Auxiliaries de Transport Commissionaires en Douane Transitaires, Agents Maritime et Aariens, November 1980.

8 GUNTON, C. E., 'The Marketing of Freight and Forwarding Services' unpublished thesis, Manchester Polytechnic.

9 See 'Freight Forwarders' Jordan & Sons (Surveys) Ltd. Annual series and 'Freight Forwarders' Intercompany Comparisons, September 1980.

10 BAXTER, R. E. and ALLERA, S. V., 'Transport and the Challenge of Structural Change', 8th Int. Symposium on Theory and Practice in Transport Economics Istanbul, September 1979.

11 LEP GROUP LTD, Annual Report, y.e. 31.12.79.

12 JORDANS 'Britain's Top 1,000 Private Companies 1979', Jordan & Sons (Surveys) Ltd, London, 1979), p. VL.

13 HERING, P., 'Herings IATA Top Twenty', *Airtrade*, May 1981,

p. 21, and ANON, 'IATA's Head Forwarders in 1980' *Freight Management*, November 1980, p. 8.

14   HERING P., 'Is Your Forwarder Taking You For a Ride' British Shipper, November 1980, p. 46.

15   NEDO, *Decision Making in Export Shipments*, London 1974.

16   TUDHOPE, R. A. 'The Freight Forwarder', in *Managing International Distribution* (eds Wentworth, F. and Christopher, M.) (Gower, Aldershot, 1979).

17   HEILBRON, R. and SAMWELL, S. D., *Kuehne and Nagel Ltd.* (Department of Trade, HMSO, London, 1978).

18   ANON. 'Freight Forwarders Conditions Unacceptable' Press Release 27.5.81, Freight Transport Association.

19   SCHMITHOFF, C., *Export Trade: Law and Practice of International Trade* (Stevens & Sons, London, 1980), p. 178 *et seq.*

20   DAVIES, G. J. *Freighting into the Eighties* (Maclean Hunter, London, 1978).

14
The carriers

This chapter covers the international carriers most relevant to the trader in manufactured and semi-manufactured goods. Thus the section on shipping largely ignores the bulk and tanker shipping fleets of the world, which in capacity terms, dominate that industry.

Shipping

The traditional structure of the world's shipping industry was of a large number of fiercely independent companies vying to carry both cargo and passengers around the world. As world trade developed so did the shipping industry but this expansion brought its problems. Fluctuation in demand for services and fierce competition on rates often meant low profits and an uncertain future. Out of this the Conference system was born where independent operators grouped together to offer a combined service under a common tariff.

The members of a Conference are normally operating liner services, that is ships designed to carry general cargo, including conventional and container ships. The system does not apply to bulk carriers and other types of shipping where there is no regular traffic between destinations and where the cargo can be fairly specific to a type of vessel. The shipper using the Conference services is offered a regular schedule but is unable to negotiate separately with the individual lines forming the Conference as to the tariff.

The Conference system has its critics. It is after all a

deliberate attempt by competing suppliers to avoid competing on price. Thus the system has been examined under monopoly and anti-trust legislation on both sides of the Atlantic.

In 1982 there were over fifty Conferences in existence in the UK alone. Each Conference links two specific areas on the globe, or trade as it is called. One line may be a member of more than one Conference and a line may not act within the Conference system for all of its sailings, even to the point where a port near a Conference area may be served by a Conference member acting outside the Conference tariff.

A strong argument in favour of the Conference system is that the constituent lines rarely have a monopoly on the trade they serve. 'Outsiders' frequently ply the same trade. These independents rarely offer a scheduled service and certainly not one on the same frequency as the Conference. So they compete on price and in doing so give the shipper some leverage in negotiating with the Conference and some element of choice.

However the Conference system does not afford direct price competition. A shipper is asked to sign a freight contract to restrict his shipments in that particular trade to Conference vessels. In return he receives a loyalty discount, about 9% of the total rate.

The Conferences police their systems rigorously trying to ensure that signatories do not ship by outsiders and that individual lines keep to their agreements on common pricing. The problem of policing is made difficult because of the ease in which control of freight can be altered by changing the terms of trade. For example a consignor who is a signatory would be obliged to use the Conference if he sold CIF. If his consignee was not a signatory and the terms changed to ex-works then the same traffic could be switched to an outsider.

Over the years many Conferences have assimilated outsiders into their system but recent changes in the structure of the liner trades have made this more difficult. The 1970s saw a rapid growth in the fleets of those countries not previously associated with having large merchant fleets. Two types of country were involved, developing nations and the Eastern bloc. Between 1967 and 1976 the registered tonnage of the Russian fleet of non-bulk shipping increased 102%. Bulgarian and Rumanian increases were 118 and 250% respectively, although from a much lower base. Out of the developing nations Iranian and Kuwaiti figures are the most spectacular with growths of 835% and 1,045%. By 1976 over 25% of the world supply of non-bulk capacity was under the control of third world and Eastern bloc fleets.

These points were made in an analysis of the market for liner shipping by Dicer and Sentell of the University of Tennessee.[1] They argue that the relative newcomers to world shipping often work towards non-profit goals. Certainly Eastern bloc shipping lines are well placed to work within totally different cost criteria to those constraining western companies. The acquisition of foreign currency is an adequate motive for the operation of state controlled shipping.

Third world countries have long been concerned about their trade being carried in foreign vessels. British carriers, for example, have always been active in cross-trading, that is carrying goods between two countries neither of which is Britain itself. Countries such as Kuwait have taken the opportunity to use their oil wealth to invest in their own shipping and establish an industry which will continue to function after their oil resources are depleted.

The United Nations Conference on Trade and Development (UNCTAD) took steps to ensure that more of a country's trade could be carried by right in their own vessels. They sponsored the so-called 40:40:20 rule under which 40% of any trade was to be carried by the ships of the two countries with 20% left for cross-traders.

Dicer and Sentell have modelled the effect of having the two types of shipping competing in the same market (Figure 34).

The market in total is represented by the full line TS (Total Supply) but this is a combination of two components, the OCS line, representing the ordinary cost determined schedule for western fleets and the SCS line.

The SCS line describes the relationship between capacity and rates for the state sector. It represents the reality that the capacity can be offered at very low rates but that increases in capacity are not readily forthcoming at higher rates.

The OCS line, describing the capacity/rates relationship of

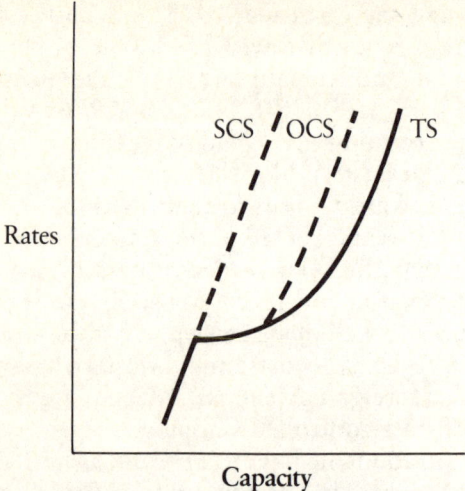

Figure 34   Supply of ocean transport capacity under conditions of market penetration by state-controlled shipping.

the western fleets, shows that at low capacity a minimum rate is still required to operate vessels. Capacity is more responsive to demand to the point where additional capacity can only be encouraged by much higher rates.

The combined line TS shows what happens when these two sectors compete in the same market. When capacity demanded is low the state controlled sector, being able to operate at what are technically uneconomic rates, attracts the cargo available. At higher capacities the immediate capacity of the state fleets is absorbed and the rest taken up by western fleets to the point where they need to see rates rise significantly before additional capacity is available. Only when this second elbow in the curve is reached does it become a seller's market.

Dicer and Sentell argue that state fleets will continue to grow even during a world slump because their motives do not require an economic return.

The outlook for western fleets does not appear to be very favourable. These pressures on rates have also had their effects on the Conference system.

Whether one accepts the view of shipping Conferences as

cartels or not it is true that lines would not have come together if they did not consider it to be in their own interests. A problem with a Conference is that rates have to be set to suit the weaker members. This restricts the ability of the Conference to compete with outsiders on price.

Faced with internal divisions and outside competition many lines have resorted to unofficial arrangements with the larger shippers or have left the Conference system. This fragmentation is likely to continue with a greater free-for-all on rates until only the stronger lines survive. Unfortunately 'strength' could not only imply efficiency but also the availability of State resources to subsidize rates. One view is that there is no long-term future for the Conference system, another that whoever they are, the stronger lines will eventually see it to their advantage to adopt the Conference structure.

The 1970s and 1980s saw considerable technical changes in shipping. The previous decade had seen the innovation of containerization but the changes in ship design in this later era were accelerated by the harsh economic situation after the oil crises and the economic recession which followed. Larger ships became relatively more economic. Few individual lines could afford to purchase such vessels. If all had done so the increase in capacity would have swamped an already over-supplied market. Yet shipping lines are by tradition fiercely independent, many still retaining the family control started by their founders centuries earlier.

The inevitable conclusion was a growth in the number of consortia who jointly operated vessels but sold their services separately in the market place. Many lines became closer to the NVOCC (non-vessel owning carriers) who, as forwarders, had seen the opportunities for owning their own containers and offering a door-to-door service using capacity on Conference and non-Conference vessels.

The buyer is now faced with an array of shipping services. Container and conventional shipping still compete but, within the container services, NVOCC, consortia, partnerships, and totally independent lines also compete. Conference vies with non-Conference service.

The advent of the larger vessel has had one more effect on

shipping services. It is less economic for the larger vessel to make a number of stops in each country. In Europe, lines have tended to concentrate on certain large ports on the Continental coast. Moving freight, especially containers, to these points has become a growth industry, introducing yet another link in the distribution chain.

Specialist services

There are a great many specialist types of ship, of which two types of service bear individual mention. The Roll-on Roll-off, RoRo, ship was used traditionally to carry road and rail units across short sea routes. However deep sea RoRo services, either in total or combined with container and conventional traffic, have found markets in the movement of road vehicles from manufacturing countries to their markets and for dealing with container and other traffic to underdeveloped countries where the port facilities leave much to be desired. The RoRo trailer is easily offloaded at a conventional quay while the container needs special equipment in good working order.

There are many advantages to the idea of utilizing canals and other waterways linked to deep-sea services. Canals were the major way of transporting goods before the railways and the internal combustion engine. The infrastructure therefore exists to build upon. European countries such as Germany and Holland move significant proportions of their domestic freight by barge.

Two systems were developed in the 1960s to enable two waterway systems to be linked by a seagoing vessel without having to unload the cargo. LASH (Lighter Aboard Ship) for deep-sea and BACAT (Barge Aboard Catamaran) have already found limited acceptance and the concept could be of increasing importance in the movement of bulk commodities with the developments recently in canal systems in a number of countries.

Airfreight

Prior to the Second World War the movement of 'cargo' by air was largely restricted to the carriage of mail. During the 1960s and 1970s different aircraft design with larger cargo hold capacities saw airfreight competing vigorously for a larger share of many types of particularly high value cargo. Airfreight now accounts for about 20% of the value of trade, but less than 1% of tonnage. The advantages of airfreight include speed and greater security. A TDC analysis can demonstrate how a company's entire product range can be distributed by air.

Aircraft can often accept very large consignments but the typical airfreight is still the small parcel. Table 8 shows the weight spectrum of airfreight from one survey.

Table 8
Weight profile for airfreight.
Source: *Civil Aviation Authority report CAP 401*

Weight of individual consignments (kg)	Total number of consignments	% of grand total	Average weight of individual consignment (kg)
0– 45	221,173	69.1	15
46– 500	85,278	26.6	166
501–2,500	11,763	3.7	1,063
Over 2,500	1,772	0.6	7.028

This profile of consignments makes it difficult for an airline, concentrating on the passenger side of its business, to offer a full freight service. Traditionally the airfreight industry has relied almost exclusively on the airfreight forwarder to provide them with a consolidation of consignments, often pre-loaded into unit load devices (igloos) ready for handling in and out of an aircraft relatively quickly so as not to delay a passenger flight carrying cargo or to make best use of a freighter's time.

Airfreight has been the Cinderella of the airline industry. The marketing of airfreight was largely left to the airfreight forwarder while the airlines concentrated on the passenger trade. Nevertheless a substantial volume of airfreight travels by freighter and freight provides approximately 10%–20% of the typical airline's total revenue.

Modern passenger aircraft, with their wide-bodied design, have the capacity for some 12–15 tonnes of 'belly hold' cargo. Some airlines have converted some passenger capacity to freight in 'combi' aircraft. The capacity of a pure freighter ranges up to the 100 tonne capacity of the freighter version of the Boeing 747.

Entry into the airfreight market as a carrier is intensely regulated worldwide despite the move by America to deregulate its own industry. There are few companies who are specialist freight carriers.

The shipper is often limited to the use of the large national airlines, normally via an airfreight forwarder. Basic airfreight rates are determined by IATA or by government regulation. IATA license the airforwarder and their hold over the airline industry has been criticized. They do in effect represent the airlines rather than airline customers or even their respective governments. Nevertheless the existence of IATA does also aid the shipper by, for example, easing the movement of freight which has to travel with more than one carrier. The IATA airway bill ensures that costs can be determined in total rather than as a series of individual charges.

The tragedy of airfreight is the low use of the mode for regular traffic because a company has analysed its distribution system and calculated an advantage for using air from a total distribution cost analysis. Airfreight still tends to be used for one-off and small consignments.

Courier services

Courier services could be considered as an airfreight service but the area deserves separate mention. The original concept is for an individual to travel on a regular airflight carrying items of no declarable value from one country to another. Such a service is normally offered from desk to desk with small vans or motorbikes acting as the collect and delivery mode.

The service has a particular value in moving documentation of all types. It is faster than a mail service, but more expensive.

Apart from a shipping department looking to move documents, courier services have been successful in attracting the custom of banks, finance houses and the head offices of large companies.

In many countries the mail service has a statutory monopoly on the movement of mail. Whether a courier service is technically a mail service or not has been argued at some length but the courier companies are now strongly promoting their services world-wide. As with the air forwarder few couriers have a world-wide coverage. Many items will be swopped between services.

The courier concept has now developed to the carriage of freight although the price structure is much higher than for regular airfreight. This slows the non-declarable documentation so many consignment courier services treat that side of their business in an almost traditional airfreight manner using belly-hold capacity in passenger aircraft.

The distinction between courier, airfreight and even fast surface freight has become blurred with the latter offering prepaid envelopes to shippers for the carriage of small consignments or documents.

Rail services

The trend world-wide has been for the railways to lose freight business to road haulage. Rail has been left with the role of longhaul carriage and large-volume, high-density commodities such as steel and coal.

Potentially rail could be used much more by the shipper. Rail's problem is its poor image for reliability and the need to employ more than one mode to move goods from buyer to seller via a railhead. Rail freight rates are often well below those of road but the twin problems of inflexibility and unreliability have been sufficient to limit their involvement in the movement of goods. International railfreight falls into two categories, where rail is the dominant mode or where rail is used to complete a movement by sea.

Railways outside America tend to be nationally owned and to be limited within national frontiers. Differences in rolling stock; gauges, tunnel clearances and the like have added to the problems of forging truly international services. In Europe Intercontainer represents the combined interests of the railways of more than 20 countries. They organize through freight trains running to published schedules, linking the various national services one to another and to the major ports. Intercontainer normally offer local road services from their terminals. Interfrigo is a similar consortium concerned with refrigerated rail transport with over 20 European members.

Although the various national and international railways market domestic and international services directly, many forwarders retail rail services and have their own specialist equipment operating on the railways, ranging from tankers to car transporters. Special wagons, from manufacturers such as VTG, are available to take advantage of the high weights that can be moved by rail.

The movement of containers nationally is often co-ordinated by a single company, who may be a subsidiary of the national railways. This compares with the situation in America with its twenty and more separate companies who still, normally, offer a full door-to-door service.

Railways are involved in moving containers, conventional cargo and bulk commodities to and from the ports. They are therefore part of an intermodal chain. A growth area in recent years has been in 'piggyback' services where a road trailer is loaded on to a railwagon. This type of service combines the flexibility of road with the longhaul economy of rail.

Rail's future as a mode seems to lie in two directions, as part of an intermodal chain for other services (in carrying trailers and containers) and in its own right if it can solve its service problems and convince its customers that it has done so.

Since Napoleonic times there has been talk of a permanent link between Britain and continental Europe. A low-cost solution is a rail-based tunnel carrying cars and lorries on railwaggons. Any rail-based tunnel would produce an expansion in British usage of rail in export and import traffic. There would be a need for large terminals to handle the transfer of cargo to, and from, road to the point where the entire structure of the freight industry could change.

Another possibility in the long term is for rail to gain from both environmental pressures against road-based traffic and the prospects of a decline in oil and oil-based fuels. Rail is better able to use a number of fuel sources either directly or via their conversion into electricity. These possibilities mean that, whatever the typical shipper's view is of railfreight now, the potential for rail has to be constantly reviewed.

Road services

Within the congested and highly developed markets of Europe international road haulage has provided the main transport capacity as trade volumes have increased. Road services are often referred to as TIR, (Transport International Routier) acknowledging the international convention on through lorry movements which allows a vehicle, approved by its national transport authority, to travel between customs points.

Essentially each vehicle has to be able to be sealed so that a load cannot be tampered with until unsealed at a customs point. Although a rigid-sided vehicle is ideal for this purpose the typical TIR vehicle has a soft cover which can be fully held by a single hawser.

The restrictions on the use of road vehicles include limits on their payload, normally expressed as weight per axle as well as total weight including the weight of the vehicle. The normal 12 metre trailer is similar in capacity to a 40 ft container in volume and limited to between 20 and 30 tonnes in weight depending on the country.

Operators distinguish between unaccompanied and accompanied services. With the latter a driver travels with the trailer and usually the tractor for any intermediate journey, such as on a ferry or piggyback service. The increased cost is justified by having a representative of the operator available to deal with any formalities that might otherwise have delayed the load.

Another factor distinguishing different types of service is whether a load consists of goods from more than one consignor. Full load rates are naturally lower than groupage rates. In between some companies refer to part load services, which offer lower rates for those moderate consignments that can form the base load for a groupage service.

The TIR convention has been partially superseded in Europe by the T form system which relates to the movement of goods within the EEC. The European TIR market is highly fragmented. Many operators refer to themselves as 'forwarders' while many genuine forwarders exist who do not own or lease vehicles but who hire the services of owner/drivers or place business with TIR operators. The market is limited to an extent by a system of permits. A permit, issued by a national government, limits the owner to a certain number of transits.

Some large operators exist but, until recently, these tended to concentrate on the full load contract end of the market. The norm for a groupage operator/forwarder is still to form an agreement with a similar company in each market served and offer a combined service marketed in each country solely under the name of the domiciled company. The larger companies have offices in many major centres but rarely offer a totally self-contained service.

It is rarely clear to the buyer what kind of service he is buying. At one extreme the transport firm may be acting as a traditional forwarder, having no services of his own and placing his client's goods with a number of carriers. At the other extreme the carrier has his own international services operating daily between his own international depots and offering complete coverage of, e.g., the European market.

During the 1970s and 1980s European TIR companies challenged the European airfreight industry on the carriage of time-sensitive goods. Such companies tended to specialize on smaller consignments than the traditional road groupage carriers, hence the expression 'fast parcels market'. The client in his turn paid more for the higher level of service but generally less than for airfreight.

Thus within one sector of the freight market, road haulage, the breadth of choice is almost as wide as in the entire freight market. 'Send it by road' becomes as anomalous a statement as 'send it anyway you like'. The shipper has to be assessing constantly exactly what cost/service package he is being offered by competing hauliers.

Postal services

Few textbooks acknowledge the importance of post as a 'freight mode' yet each year as many consignments leave Britain by post as by all other means of transport put together. Most postal 'consignments' will be private correspondence rather than goods but the parcels service offered by the various national postal services can be of value to the shipper of small consignments.

The image of postal services is of bureaucracy and delay. In reality such services are quite extensive and often unique. In some sectors, particularly courier services, postal services compete directly.

Weight limit is the main problem facing the exporter looking to make wider use of the post. Most countries have a limit of 10 kg although some allow up to 20 kg. Another factor is whether the exporter has to deliver his goods into the postal service instead of the goods being collected, as is the normal practice in the freight industry.

Conversely postal rates are often well below commercial freight rates where carriers tend to penalize small consignments with high minimum charges. Documentation is often simpler for postal freight. Customs charges can be prepaid. Customs formalities for goods up to a certain value are often minimal. Some services allow for cash on delivery.

Postal services between countries span a range of different service levels. Premium services are specially handled in each country and move predominantly by air. Economy services move by surface. Some premium services limit the value of goods that can be carried.

Overlap between transport modes

In many respects it is misleading to analyse the international distribution industry by mode. A more appropriate method would be to analyse all services between individual markets in terms of their frequency of service, speed and reliability and cost. Most services overlap with other services both inside and outside their own mode. A shipper may not know that a container has been moved by rail rather than road. He may even take the view that it is his forwarder's responsibility to select the most relevant method of moving his goods at the time of shipment.

It is better to think in terms of route-modes rather than individual services and different modes. Any destination served regularly should be researched for every route mode combination. Some companies offer intermodel services within one operation. Others do not but the advent of unit loads makes this less of a problem.

It is all too easy, and somewhat dangerous, to accept a stereotype of a particular freight mode and to disregard a service of potential cost saving or service improvement – something of course an international logistics manager would never do!

Keypoints

1 The structure of the world shipping industry is ever changing. The Conference system, much criticized, may be expected to come under further attack, perhaps to the point where a new system will evolve.

2 Overcapacity in world fleets and the pricing policies of third world and Eastern European fleets will dominate rates during the 1980s.

3 Airfreight is generally used for smaller, high value consignments and urgent despatches by exporters rather than for general freight to optimize delivery times and stock levels.

4 Rail freight has suffered from the image of rail as being unreliable. It is nevertheless a worthy competitor to both sea and road.

5 Road freight, because of its flexibility, is the dominant mode for land transits.

6 Postal services are too frequently ignored as a means of serving an export market.

References and further reading

1 DICER, G. N. and SENTELL, G. D. 'Changing Maritime Transport Patterns in the 80's' in 'International Logistics' *Int. J. Phys Dist. Mat. Mgmt.* Vol. II, 5/6, 1981.

CHANNON, D. F. 'The International Shipping Industry' case study. Manchester Business School MBS/BP/46 Distributed by the Case Clearing House of Great Britain 382–034–1.

THOMAS MEADOWS LTD *Understanding the Freight Business* (London, 1979).

Index